MW00411706

50

American Serial Killers You've Probably Never Heard Of

Volume Four

Robert Keller

Please Leave Your Review of This Book At
http://bit.ly/kellerbooks

ISBN-13: 978-1535138437

ISBN-10: 1535138432

© 2016 by Robert Keller

robertkellerauthor.com

All rights reserved.

No part of this publication may be copied or reproduced in any format, electronic or otherwise, without the prior, written consent of the copyright holder and publisher. This book is for informational and entertainment purposes only and the author and publisher will not be held responsible for the misuse of information contain herein, whether deliberate or incidental.

Much research, from a variety of sources, has gone into the compilation of this material. To the best knowledge of the author and publisher, the material contained herein is factually correct. Neither the publisher, nor author will be held responsible for any inaccuracies.

Table of Contents

4   Robert Keller

Robert Arguelles

They say that fatherhood changes a man, but few changes can have been as dramatic as that experienced by Robert Arguelles. In May 1996, while serving a prison term for child molestation, Arguelles received a letter informing him that a former girlfriend had conceived his child. Shortly after, Arguelles contacted prison authorities and said that he wanted to confess to a series of murders committed in Salt Lake City, Utah, four years earlier.

"I realize these girls were just little girls like mine," he said. "I started to understand just how much it would hurt to have someone do what I had done."

The murders that Arguelles was referring to had occurred in the Utah state capital in the winter of 1992, shortly after Arguelles had been paroled from a prison term for attempted murder and aggravated assault. He had also previously served time for the rape of a ten-year-old girl.

Arguelles was 30 years old and working as a laborer at a metals processing plant when the murders began. His first victim was Margo Bond, a 42-year-old high school janitor who he encountered while he was trawling the school grounds, looking for teenaged victims. Bond was sexually assaulted and strangled to death.

Three weeks later, Arguelles saw 13-year-old Stephanie Blundell walking to school. He stopped and offered the girl a ride, then drove her to an isolated spot where he raped and strangled her.

Barely a week passed before Arguelles struck again. This time, he picked up 14-year-old Tuesday Roberts and 16-year-old Lisa Martinez from a bus stop and offered them a ride to the mall. Once inside his vehicle, the girls were overpowered and handcuffed together. Arguelles first tried to rape Lisa, but when she resisted he stabbed her to death with a wood chisel, delivering over 40 blows in a frenzied attack. He then sexually assaulted Tuesday before strangling her to death. The girls' bodies were buried at a pig farm.

Shortly after the double murder, Arguelles was arrested for sexual assault and eventually sentenced to another long prison term. Now, a tearful, repentant Arguelles was fully prepared to pay for his crimes. He wanted the death penalty, he said, preferably by firing squad and if possible without a hood. Utah is one of only three states that utilizes this form of execution, allowing the condemned prisoner to choose between it and lethal injection. Most pick the latter.

On May 12, 1997, Arguelles – who had spent virtually his entire adult life behind bars – entered guilty pleas to each of four charges of first-degree murder. On June 20, Third District Court Judge David Young sentenced him to die by firing squad. Arguelles immediately stated his intention to fight any appeals on his behalf. He wanted to die as quickly as possible, he said.

However, his behavior during the trial, spitting, and screaming profanities, had raised questions as to his sanity. As a result, his execution, scheduled for June 27, 2003, was stayed until his competency could be determined.

Arguelles, meanwhile, was deteriorating mentally. After the stay of execution, he tried to hang himself with a pillowcase. When that failed, he began habitually eating his own feces.

In the end, Arguelles got the death penalty he so desperately wanted, although it was not the one sanctioned by the state of Utah. Hospitalized with an intestinal blockage in November 2003, he refused medical treatment. He passed away quietly on November 15 and was pronounced dead at 17:27. He was 41 years old.

Joseph Baldi

Between September 1970 and June 1972, the residents of Queens, New York, were terrorized by a deadly prowler. The man appeared out of the dark like a phantom, entering homes and slashing at his female victims while they slept. Nothing was stolen and no obvious attempt was made at sexual assault. It seemed the intruder's sole purpose was to inflict injury and death.

The first attack occurred on September 20, 1970, when Areti Koularmanis was stabbed to death in her bed. Over the next 18 months, the slasher struck four more times, his victims suffering serious knife wounds but escaping with their lives. Then, on March 19, 1972, he killed again, stabbing to death 17-year-old Camille Perniola as she slept.

This latest murder threw the borough of Queens into panic, and as the community cowered in fear, the police stepped up patrols in the area in a desperate effort to catch the killer. It did no good. On April 13, 1972, 21-year-old Clara Toriello was killed in her bed, bringing the death toll to three. And still, the police had no clue as to who they were looking for.

After a brief hiatus, the prowler was back on June 13, reaching through an open window to inflict deep slash wounds to the face of a sleeping teenager. The girl survived. Two days later, in the early hours of June

15, another Queens woman woke to find a man climbing through her bedroom window. She started screaming, causing the intruder to flee.

The next victim was not so lucky. Sixteen-year-old Deborah Januszko was hacked and slashed to death in a Jamaica, Queens, apartment on June 17.

Three days after the Januszko murder, Detective Donald Palmer spotted a man walking furtively through the early morning dark in the vicinity of the crime scene. The man identified himself as Joseph Baldi and said that he was attending a trade school in the area. This turned out to be a lie, rousing Palmer's suspicions.

Looking into Baldi's background, the detective learned that the 31-year-old man had a lengthy rap sheet, with charges ranging from burglary to assault. He'd also been in and out of mental institutions and had nine months earlier been arrested for the attempted murder of a police officer.

Armed with this information, Palmer headed for Baldi's apartment, which as it turned out, was just fifty feet from the Januszko residence. Palmer encountered his man in the hall and told him he was investigating a homicide. The hulking, 6-foot-4, 200-pound Baldi, seemed unperturbed. He even invited the detective inside. When his answers to Palmer's questions proved unsatisfactory, the detective asked him to come down to the station. He complied without protest.

Under questioning at the precinct, Baldi surprised the interrogating officers by going into a trance-like state and re-enacting the Januszko murder, before collapsing to the floor. He subsequently confessed to all four murders and a search of his apartment turned up the collection of knives used in the attacks.

Despite his history of mental illness, Joseph Baldi was found competent to stand trial. He was found guilty on four counts of first-degree murder and sentenced to life in prison.

Jack Barron

On June 8, 1992, Norma Paget received a frantic call from her son-in-law, Jack Barron. "You gotta get over here quick!" Barron shouted down the line.

"Why?" Norma asked, startled. When Barron didn't reply, she repeated, "Why?"

"Irene's dead," Barron said tersely, before hanging up.

Barely able to believe what she'd heard, Norma Paget and her husband, Jack, sped across town to the home their daughter Irene shared with Jack Barron and the couple's two young children. They arrived to find the scene cordoned off by police, an ambulance parked at the curb. Barron was nowhere to be seen, but a detective informed the Pagets that their 34-year-old daughter had been found dead in the home's master bedroom.

The police immediately suspected foul play. A neighbor had found Irene, sitting propped up in bed. There were no obvious signs of violence on the body, but a pillow smeared with her make-up suggested that she might have been suffocated.

It was all down to what the Sacramento County Coroner's Office would determine as cause of death. Asphyxial death by deliberate suffocation or smothering is difficult to prove and frequently leaves no signs. The coroner couldn't be sure and therefore entered cause of death as "undetermined."

Jack Barron, of course, denied any involvement in Irene's death. He'd been at work when her body was discovered and assured the authorities that she'd been very much alive when he'd left the house. At the funeral, he appeared distraught and garnered much sympathy.

Alone now, and with two young children to care for, Barron invited one of his co-workers, Starla Hayes, to move into his home with her two children. The plan was that they would help each other in caring for the children, but a sexual relationship soon developed. A couple of months later, Starla moved out, unable to cope with Barron's controlling personality.

Within weeks of Hayes' departure, a babysitter found four-year-old Jeremy Barron unconscious in his bed. An ambulance was called but arrived to find the toddler dead at the scene. As in Irene's case, deliberate suffocation was suspected but could not be proven. Barron insisted that his son had suffered from hereditary heart disease.

In the wake of Jeremy's death, Barron's surviving child, three-year-old Ashley, was examined by a pediatric cardiologist. The doctor found a slight irregularity in the child's heartbeat but said that it was nothing serious and that Ashley was in no danger. He did, however, ask Barron to schedule follow-up appointments, which Barron never kept.

Eighteen months later, Ashley was dead in startlingly similar circumstances to her brother. Despite the findings of the cardiologist, Barron was adamant that she'd suffered heart failure and the coroner could not prove otherwise.

Barron next moved in with his mother, Roberta. The two had always enjoyed a close relationship, but Roberta evidently found her son a difficult housemate. Within months, she'd confided in a friend that she was going to ask Jack to move out. She never got the chance.

On February 27, 1995, Barron phoned the police to report that he'd found his mother lying dead in her bedroom. Detectives arrived to find a familiar scene. Roberta was propped up in bed, dressed in pajamas. The body bore no signs of violence and it was later determined that she'd died of asphyxiation.

But luck had finally run out for Barron. Unlike his Sacramento counterpart, the Solano County coroner declared the death a homicide and Barron found himself under arrest. In the wake of the ruling, Sacramento reopened their cases and also ruled the deaths of Irene, Jeremy, and Ashley to be homicides.

Jack Barron went on trial in April 2000. Despite his protestations of innocence, he was sentenced to three consecutive life terms without the possibility of parole.

Joseph Briggen

Before he achieved lasting infamy as a mass murderer, Joseph Briggen's singular claim to fame in Sierra Morena, California, was the quality of his prize Berkshire hogs. Not a year went by where Briggen's hogs didn't walk away with the top prizes at the state fair in Sacramento. And when envious competitors enquired about the secret of his success, he'd always provide the same, enigmatic answer. "It's all in the feeding," he'd say, a mischievous glint in his eye.

Briggen was born in northern California in 1850, the product of farming stock. Following in the Briggen tradition, he took over the family spread on his father's death. But the land was far from fertile. The crops invariably failed entirely or were of such poor quality that they were unfit for human consumption. If it hadn't been for Briggen's beloved hogs, he may well have given up farming altogether.

Those hogs were his pride and joy and Briggen made sure that they were well cared for, even if keeping help on his farm was a constant cause of frustration, a fact he often bemoaned to his neighbors.

Briggen generally recruited his workers from the shiftless transients in the Embarcadero district of San Francisco. He made regular trips to the city, and although he offered no wages, only board and lodging, there were plenty of takers. To a homeless man, hungry and living on the street, the promise of three squares a day and a soft bed must have seemed attractive. That is, until they arrived at the Briggen farmstead.

Briggen required a lot of his workers, setting them to work at backbreaking tasks and allowing them very little rest. Once they saw the nature of the work they were required to perform, the workers usually insisted on payment, a demand Joseph Briggen was neither prepared, nor able, to entertain.

Sometimes Briggen's employees lasted a week or two, sometimes only a day before they were gone – run off, he'd tell anyone who bothered to ask. The truth was rather more sinister. Whenever money was demanded, Briggen settled the dispute quickly and decisively, dispatching the man with a bullet to the head. He'd then dismember the body, grind up the flesh and feed it to his hogs.

At first, this method of disposal may have been just a convenient way of disposing of a murder victim. But over time, Briggen came to genuinely believe that his hogs needed to feast on human flesh in order to reach their peak condition. It was then that he began to make his weekly "shopping trips" to San Francisco.

The victims he chose were rarely missed and Briggen might have continued indefinitely had he not become sloppy. In early 1902, he picked a young man named Steven Korad off the streets and brought him to Sierra Morena. After Korad had put in his first day's work, he retired to his quarters. Checking out the room before turning in, Korad found two severed fingers lying under the bed. He immediately fled, working his way through the dark to report his discovery to the police.

Investigators arrived at the Briggen farm the following morning and a search of the premises turned up enough skulls and human bones to account for at least 12 victims.

Briggen was tried, found guilty of murder and sentenced to life in prison. He survived only a few months in San Quentin before he died. The identity and final tally of his victims remains a mystery.

Rickey H. Brogsdale

Over a period of seven weeks, between September and October 1987, Washington D.C. was terrorized by a serial shooter who seemed to derive pleasure from stalking lone women or couples, spying on them in their homes and then firing through open windows with a .22-caliber weapon.

The "Peeping Tom Shooter" first drew attention on September 5, 1987, when he shot at a woman as she stood in the bedroom of her home. A slew of attacks followed although none resulted in fatalities. Then, after the sniper shot and injured an off-duty policewoman on October 15, the police eventually went public to warn the community.

It did nothing to discourage the shooter. Three attacks followed in quick succession, the third (and eighth overall) resulting in the first fatality, a 35-year-old Watts woman killed by a .22-caliber bullet fired from outside her home.

Several hours after the shooting, metro police officers stopped and questioned a man found lurking in the area. The man identified himself as Rickey Brogsdale, age 26. He could not provide a reason for being in the area and his nervous glances towards a nearby clump of bushes caused the officers to conduct a search there. They turned up a .22-caliber pistol.

Taken in for questioning, Brogsdale readily admitted to the "Peeping Tom" attacks, even adding three more fatal shootings that the police had not yet connected to the series.

Investigators soon learned that Brogsdale had recently been paroled from a period of incarceration for carrying an unlicensed pistol. Since his release, five months earlier, he'd been in trouble on a number of occasions, including for indecent exposure and the molestation of a 10-year-old girl. On each occasion, the authorities had failed to revoke his parole.

But the charges facing Brogsdale now were much more serious and he seemed to revel in his newfound infamy. According to Brogsdale's confession, his first murder took place on September 5, the same day the "Peeping Tom" shootings began. The victim was Myers Jackson, a man who (according to Brogsdale) had tried to rape Brogsdale's mother in 1976.

The following day, Brogsdale carried out another revenge killing. Calling on the apartment of a man who he accused of murdering his sister, Brogsdale opened fire. Twenty-eight-year-old Steven Wilson died at the scene. His girlfriend was seriously wounded.

Brogsdale's third murder had nothing to do with revenge. On September 20, he hid in some bushes beside a bike path. When teenager Angela Shaw passed, he pounced on her, strangled her into unconsciousness, raped her, and then shot her to death with a .22-caliber weapon.

Shortly after the murder, the police received an anonymous call directing them to the scene. Beside the body, lay a macabre note. It read: "I raped and killed your friend, Angela Shaw. You can find her on the bike path behind Marbury Plaza."

Brogsdale later tried to rescind his confession to the Shaw murder, but the note, in his handwriting, provided strong evidence. Nonetheless, he would never be tried for the murder.

The killings of Steven Wilson and Yvonne Watts were another matter. Convicted on these charges, Brogsdale was sentenced to a prison term of 63 years to life.

Curtis Don Brown

Eight young women were missing in the space of just three months and police in Tarrant County, Texas, were certain that they had a serial killer on their streets. The first to disappear was Catherine Davis, an aspiring model who went missing on September 30, 1984. Then, on October 22, Cindy Heller, a former beauty queen and a student at Texas Christian University, disappeared. Cindy had stopped to help a stranded motorist that night and ended up having a few drinks with her. The two parted at around 11:30 p.m. Heller was never seen alive again.

On January 5, 1985, a group of children playing near a creek on the TCU campus spotted something floating in the water. It turned out to be a headless corpse (later identified as Cindy Heller). The police were called and conducted a search of the area. Two hours later, they found another corpse lying nearby, that of 20-year-old waitress, Lisa Griffin.

Another body was discovered on March 23, 1985. Eighteen-year-old Sharyn Killsback, a member of the Oglala Sioux tribe, had disappeared on March 15. A plumber discovered her corpse in a south Arlington storm drain. Her face and the front of her body were caked in mud and she had a rope around her neck. Cause of death was determined to be strangulation. She'd also been raped.

Two months later, on May 30, Terece Gregory, 29, was found floating in the Trinity River. She'd last been seen leaving the Caravan of Dreams, a nightclub in downtown Fort Worth. She'd been raped and shot.

The Fort Worth authorities had in the meanwhile assembled a task force. But the investigation soon ran into trouble. Most of the bodies were in an advanced state of decomposition, making it impossible to lift usable physical evidence. Crime scene technicians were able to obtain semen from Killsback and Gregory, but without a suspect to match it to, it got the police no closer to catching their killer.

In 1986, a couple of patrolmen encountered a man walking along a Fort Worth street. The man was carrying a towel and his movements appeared furtive, causing the officers to pull over and question him. A subsequent search of his person turned up two purses wrapped in the towel. Unable to provide a satisfactory answer as to where they'd come from, the man was taken into custody. He was later identified as Curtis Don Brown.

The following day, officers went looking for the owners of the two purses and found one of them, a 51-year-old nurse named Jewel Woods, dead. She'd been raped and strangled, her body hidden in some bushes close to her apartment building. Curtis Brown was subsequently charged with the murder, found guilty, and sentenced to life in prison.

In the months that followed, the investigation into the Fort Worth murders continued to flounder. Eventually, the task force was dismantled, the officers reassigned to more pressing cases. The killings had stopped anyway, and it was assumed that the killer had died, moved away, or been convicted of an unrelated crime. There would be no progress in the case for another 20 years.

In February 2005, cold case investigators were looking into the spate of mid-eighties murders when they got a hit on the CODIS database. Semen from Terece Gregory's body was matched to convicted felon, Curtis Don Brown. A few days later, they got another match, this time linking Brown to the murder of Sharyn Killsback.

Confronted with the evidence, Brown struck a deal, offering a full confession to the Gregory and Killsback murders in exchange for a life sentence in each case.

Brown has never been charged with any of the other Fort Worth murders. But he remains the prime suspect in eighteen homicides committed in Tarrant County while he was active there.

Joseph Bryan

Among the most vile of serial killers are those who prey on children. One of this breed, Joseph F. Bryan, was born in Camden, New Jersey in 1939. Not much is known of Bryan's childhood and upbringing, so it's difficult to determine what fueled his fixation with young boys. However, by 1958, when Bryan was 19, he was already on police radars after he kidnapped two boys, tied them to a tree, and sexually molested them.

Committed to a mental hospital, Bryan was diagnosed as a schizophrenic, and a dangerous one at that. During one therapy session, he calmly informed his psychiatrist that he was aroused by seeing little boys "tied up and screaming." Astoundingly, given these admissions, he was released. He enlisted in the navy but was soon discharged after evidence of mental illness surfaced.

Bryan showed up next in Nevada, where he was convicted on charges of burglary and auto theft and sent to prison. He was paroled on January 20, 1964.

Just over a month later, 7-year-old John Robinson disappeared while riding his bicycle near his home in Mount Pleasant, South Carolina. FBI agents investigating the disappearance heard from two local farmers about a car they had helped pull from a ditch in the early hours of February 28. The driver had been traveling with a young boy. The farmers had been suspicious of him. One of them had noted down the license plate number.

The vehicle was traced to Joseph F. Bryan who, agents learned, had spent a couple of nights in a nearby motel. When John Robinson's bike was found in some weeds not far from where the car had been bogged down, an APB went out for Bryan's arrest. Despite a massive search, he somehow slipped the net.

On March 23, 1964, seven-year-old Lewis Wilson Jr. vanished from a school in St. Petersburg, Florida. As searchers began combing the area in a fruitless search for the missing boy, news came of a gruesome discovery. The skeletal remains of a young child had been found in a marsh near Hallandale. The body was naked except for shoes and socks. A positive identification soon followed. It was Johnny Robinson.

Now wanted for kidnapping and murder, Joseph Bryan was placed on the FBI's Most Wanted list on April 14, 1964. While a nationwide search for him was underway, 8-year-old David Wulff went missing from his home in Willingboro, New Jersey. David's whereabouts were still unknown on April 23, when another 8-year old, Dennis Burke of Humboldt, Tennessee, vanished.

April 28 finally brought a break in the case when a couple of FBI agents spotted Bryan's distinctive white Cadillac parked outside a shopping plaza in New Orleans. Bryan was arrested as he emerged from the mall, holding Dennis Burke by the hand. The child would later testify that Bryan had treated him well during their three days together.

For his part, Bryan seemed bewildered. Initially, he denied any wrongdoing, claiming that Dennis Burke had come with him willingly and that he was therefore not guilty of kidnapping. Confronted with the evidence of the other missing children, though, he broke down and confessed.

On January 12, 1965, Bryan pled guilty to federal kidnapping charges and was sentenced to life in prison.

David Bullock

David Bullock had a history of problems with the law dating back to adolescence. The native New Yorker, born November 13, 1960, clocked his first arrest in February 1977, when he was just 16. That charge was for criminal mischief and petty larceny. Five months later, he was arrested again, this time for attempted grand larceny. A guilty plea saw him committed to a juvenile delinquency center where he remained until November 1977, walking free just shy of his 17th birthday.

Bullock had learned nothing from his time inside and was in police custody again in January 1978, having been arrested for burglary. Now flagged as a juvenile offender, he spent a spell of incarceration in Goshen, New York. Over the next three years, he graduated to adult prisons, and short sentences for robbery and grand larceny. During his brief periods of freedom, he supplemented his criminal income by working as a male prostitute, a downward spiral that would lead him eventually to murder.

What exactly caused Bullock to unleash the orgy of bloodshed that he did, is unknown. What we do know is that, between December 1981 and January 1982, the fury inside David Bullock was turned on the citizens of New York, leaving at least six lives snuffed out. His only explanation, given shortly after his arrest, was that, "It's fun."

The first to die was James Weber, a 42-year-old actor shot to death without provocation as he strolled in Central Park on the evening of December 4. Nine days later, Bullock was visiting with prostitute Edwina Atkins. During sex, Bullock bragged to her about killing Weber, but she didn't believe him. In order to prove a point, he placed a pillow over her face and shot her in the head. Before leaving, he set fire to her apartment.

On December 15, Bullock propositioned 29-year-old Stephen Hassell, who took him home for sex. During the act, Bullock repeated his M.O. from the Atkins murder, pushing a pillow over Hassell's face before shooting him. Later he'd tell investigators that he'd killed Hassell to amuse himself.

For his next murder, Bullock found a victim closer to home, his roommate Michael Winley. Winley was shot in the head on December 23 and dumped in the Harlem River. His body has never been found.

The following day, Bullock attended a Christmas party and went home with 50-year-old Heriberto Morales. According to Bullock's later testimony, Morales "started messing with the Christmas tree, telling me how nice the Christmas tree was, so I shot him." He then set Morales' apartment on fire before walking away from the scene.

The five murders committed thus far had been motiveless, the victims killed purely for the amusement of the killer. However, finding himself short of cash on January 4, Bullock decided to commit a robbery.

Arming himself with a sawed-off shotgun, he set off for Mount Morris Park, where he lay in wait until he saw 28-year-old Eric Fuller approaching. The young man willingly handed over his wallet but it wasn't enough to save his life. He died in a hail of shotgun pellets.

Bullock was eventually arrested on January 15 and made no secret of the fact that he'd killed six people. In fact, he said, there might be other victims. He'd taken shots at "four or five" other people but hadn't waited around to see if he'd "got them."

Six murders were enough, though, to put him away for life, with the judge stipulating that he will never be freed.

James Canaday

It was a crime that touched many in Kings County, Washington. On the afternoon of December 17, 1968, Thomas Bowman and his pregnant, 16-year-old wife Sandra, spent time together listening to records, eating waffles and writing out their Christmas lists. Then Thomas left to work his night-shift factory job. He returned next morning to find Sandra's blood-drenched body lying face down on the bed, her hands tied behind her back. An autopsy would later determine that she'd been stabbed 57 times, many of the wounds inflicted on her clearly protruding belly. Later Thomas would find a poignant note left by Sandra before she'd retired to bed. In it, she said how much she loved him.

A diligent hunt was launched to find Sandra's killer with King County officials offering a reward for information and Thomas Bowman chipping in out of his meager savings. It came to nothing. Soon all leads had been exhausted and the trail went cold. It would remain so for over three decades.

On January 4, 1969, less than three weeks after the murder of Sandra Bowman, a man knocked on the door of an apartment occupied by 21-year-old flight attendant, Mary Annabelle Bjornson. He told her that he had car trouble and asked if he could use the phone. As soon as Bjornson allowed him in, he turned on her, produced a knife and tied her wrists with a piece of rope. He then drove her to Seward Park, where he raped and strangled her.

Three weeks later, the same man ambushed 20-year-old University of Washington junior, Lynne Carol Tuski, as she walked to her car outside a Sears store in North Seattle. She, too, was raped and strangled, her body dumped near Stevens Pass.

By the time police made an arrest in February 1969, six women had been attacked, although the other four had escaped with their lives. The suspect was a 24-year-old pipe fitter named James Canaday and he quickly confessed to the crimes before leading police to the bodies. Tried in 1969, he was sentenced to death. That sentence was commuted to life in prison after the U.S. Supreme Court declared capital punishment unconstitutional in 1972.

In 2002, the Washington State Police, like many law enforcement agencies in the country, formed a Cold Case Squad in order to look into old, unsolved cases using modern investigative techniques. One of the first they looked at was the Sandra Bowman case. Evidence from the 1968 crime scene was sent to the Washington State Patrol Crime Lab, where a DNA profile was extracted from the semen found at the scene. Submitted to the state DNA database it found an immediate match – to James Canaday, currently serving life at the Washington State Penitentiary in Walla Walla.

Seattle police detectives visited Canaday at Walla Walla in June 2004. After showing him a crime scene photograph of Sandra Bowman's brutalized body, they asked if he knew anything about the murder. Canaday hesitated, at which one of the detectives prompted him by adding that his DNA had been found at the scene. Canaday then sighed, held up his hands and said, "Yes, I killed her."

Canaday went on to explain that he'd chosen the Bowman apartment at random, knocked on the door and then forced Sandra inside and attacked her. He blamed the attack on a bitter divorce he was going through. "I had a lot of anger at myself," he said.

Canaday was sentenced to an additional life term for the murder. That will add not a day to his prison time, but at least it brought some closure to Tom Bowman who had waited 35 years to see justice done.

William Christenson

A native of Bethesda, Maryland, William Christenson first came to the attention of police in 1969, when he was charged with stabbing a teenaged girl in Washington D.C. Two years later, he was convicted of the rape of a stripper in Maryland. He served nine years for that offense, securing parole in 1980.

Following his release, Christenson adopted the name Richard Owen and moved to Canada. On April 16, 1981, he was arrested for rape in Montreal, although a plea bargain saw the charge reduced to indecent assault. He served only one year before being released.

On April 27, 1982, Montreal police were called to the apartment occupied by recent-parolee Richard Owen. Inside they found a decapitated, dismembered corpse, later identified as 27-year-old Sylvie Trudel.

As police launched a search for Christenson, the mutilated remains of 26-year-old Murielle Guay were found wrapped in trash bags at Mille-Isles, some 50 miles north of Montreal.

Although the Canadian authorities initially insisted that the two crimes were not connected, subsequent inquiries forced them to backtrack. On April 29, murder warrants were issued in the name of William Christenson.

Christenson, meanwhile, had fled back to the United States, where he called on his parents in Lancaster, Pennsylvania. The Christensons handed over $5,000 in cash to assist their son in making his getaway. (After his eventual arrest, they'd both be charged with harboring a fugitive.)

The next five months saw Christenson constantly on the move, spending time in Florida, Georgia, Kentucky, Maryland, New Jersey, New York, and Pennsylvania. By September, he was living in Scranton, New Jersey, and using the alias Stanley Holl. On September 13, 1982, the body of stripper Michelle Angiers was found in a parking lot in the nearby city of Dickson. She had been stabbed over 30 times.

Inquiries into the Angiers murder led nowhere, with the killer already having fled to Trenton. It was there, nine months later, that Christenson committed his next crime, shooting two men who he had met in a bar. Both victims survived.

December found Christenson in Philadelphia, where he used the same weapon to kill another man, Jeffrey Schrader, in a bar fight. Christenson was arrested at the scene and while he sat in jail, the police executed a search warrant on his apartment. They found a bloody mattress and a hacksaw, matted with blood and hair.

The police were unable to determine who the blood was from, and Christenson wasn't talking. They did, however, have him on the Schrader murder, and a conviction, in that case, saw him sentenced to life without parole.

Christenson was duly sent down to begin his sentence, but still, the charges kept piling up. Trenton authorities wanted him for the double shooting committed there. Montgomery County, Maryland, wanted him on rape charges. Then there were two more unsolved murders in Pennsylvania and thirteen other murder charges from jurisdictions along the eastern seaboard. All of them involved decapitation and dismemberment, leading one Pennsylvania officer to dub Christenson "an American Jack the Ripper."

On February 16, 1985, Christenson was brought to trial for the 1982 murder of Michelle Angiers. He was convicted of third-degree murder, with 20 years added to his sentence.

In August 1985, Canadian authorities closed their files on four homicides (Sylvie Trudel, Murielle Guay, plus two similar murders) citing Christenson's current life sentence.

All told, authorities believe Christenson might be responsible for 30-plus murders, making him one of the most prolific serial killers in American history.

Dellmus Colvin

It is the ultimate investigative nightmare, a killer who is always on the move, who might be on the other side of the country by the time a body is discovered, who might even have moved the entire crime scene with him. I'm talking, of course, about the phenomenon of the trucker / killer. When you think about it, the job provides the perfect cover for a serial killer along with a ready-made supply of victims, the prostitutes, or "lot lizards," who ply their trade at the myriad truck stops across the country. And so, in recent years, we've had Wayne Adam Ford, Keith Jesperson, Darren O'Neall, Robert Ben Rhodes and Sean Patrick Goble, to name just a few. To that roll of infamy can now be added, Dellmus Colvin.

Colvin was serving a prison term for rape when cold case investigators got a match that linked his DNA to the murders of two prostitutes, Melissa Weber and Jackie Simpson. Simpson, 33, was found on April 23, 2003, her body concealed under bushes near a tanning salon in Toledo, Ohio. The mother of two had been missing for three months.

Weber, 37, was discovered May 9, 2005. Her decomposed body was wrapped in a sheet and hidden under a couch at a trucking terminal.

Faced with the evidence against him, Colvin offered investigators a deal. He was prepared to confess to five homicides in exchange for the death penalty being waived.

This kind of proposal is commonplace and puts prosecutors in a difficult position. On the one hand, you have the families of the known victims, keen to see the slayer of their loved ones pay the ultimate price for his crimes. On the other, are those families who are still seeking closure, who need to know where their loved ones are buried and how they died. Because of this, prosecutors often opt to accept the deal, as they did in Colvin's case.

With the death penalty off the table, Colvin formally confessed to the murders he was accused of, as well as three others: Valerie Jones, 38, whose skeletal remains were found on January 6, 2000, at a landfill near the Ottawa River; Jacquelynn Thomas, 42, whose body was found September 2, 2000, just across the Michigan state line in Bedford Township; and Lily Summers, 43, a mother of two whose body turned up on April 8, 2002, behind an auto repair shop. All five victims had been strangled or smothered to death, their bodies wrapped in sheets and blankets, and then dumped.

The following day, Colvin admitted to a sixth murder, that of 40-year-old Dorothea Wetzel of Toledo. Her skeletal remains had been found by a man walking his dog along the Maumee River on August 5, 2000.

A seventh murder was subsequently added to the docket. Somers Point resident Donna Lee White was initially believed to have died of acute cocaine intoxication. Now Colvin came clean and admitted to deliberately overdosing her. With that, he said, the slate was clean. He'd admitted to everything. Ohio investigators are not so sure. They regard Colvin as their prime suspect in a number of other prostitute murders.

In terms of his plea agreement, Dellmus Colvin was given five consecutive life sentences without the possibility of parole.

Mary Frances Creighton

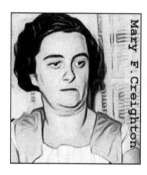

Like many serial killers, Mary Francis Creighton simply did not know
to quit while she was ahead. Already tried and acquitted in two
separate murder trials, you might have thought that Mary would have
laid low. Instead, she murdered a third victim, a crime that would
ultimately land her in the electric chair.

Born Mary Francis Avery in New Jersey in 1898, she married John
Creighton in 1920 and bore him a daughter, Ruth. In 1923, she and her
husband were arrested for the murder of her brother, Raymond Avery,
who had died after consuming a lethal dose of arsenic. The motive was
money. Raymond stood to inherit a substantial trust fund and had also
taken out a life insurance policy, with his sister named as beneficiary.

Yet, even though she was proven to have purchased substantial
amounts of arsenic in the weeks prior to Raymond's death, Mary was
acquitted of his murder. Her freedom was short-lived, however. Just
days after her acquittal, she was arrested for the murder of her mother-

in-law. In fact, both of her husband's parents had recently died under suspicious circumstances, but again the verdict came down in Mary's favor. Not long after, she relocated her family from New Jersey to Long Island, New York.

Settling in the small town of Baldwin, the Creightons soon befriended their neighbors, Everett and Ada Appelgate. This being during the Great Depression, the two couples struck on a money saving idea, and not long after, the Appelgates moved in to cohabitate with the Creightons.

Within weeks, the arrangement had taken a sordid turn, when the Creightons' pretty 15-year-old daughter, Ruth, entered into a sexual relationship with the pudgy, 37-year-old, Everett Appelgate. If that wasn't enough, the unlikely couple was sometimes joined in bed by the overweight Ada Appelgate, and on other occasions by the Applegate's 12-year-old daughter, Ada.

Mary Creighton also became Everett's lover, although she would later claim that he forced her into sex by threatening to reveal her murderous background.

In September 1936, Ada Appelgate complained of feeling ill and was examined at a local hospital before being discharged. Several days later, she was dead, her death attributed to heart failure.

Funeral arrangements were made and Ada's death might well have passed without notice outside her immediate circle. However, before the burial could take place, a stack of yellowed newspaper cuttings, documenting Mary Creighton's previous brushes with the law, was

mailed anonymously to the Nassau County District Attorney's office.
An investigation was launched, and an autopsy on Ada Appelgate
showed massive doses of arsenic in her system.

Mary was hauled in for questioning and under sustained interrogation
eventually confessed to killing Ada, naming Everett as her accomplice.
It was a story she'd change many times.

Mary Frances Creighton and Everett Appelgate went on trial at the
Nassau County Criminal Court on January 12, 1936. The trial, with its
sordid details of child sex and murder, was a sensation, especially
when Mary and Everett each tried to finger the other as the perpetrator.
It did neither of them any good, they were both found guilty and
sentenced to die in the electric chair.

Over the next few months, several appeals were filed, but all failed and
a date of July 16 was set for the executions. As that date approached,
Mary's physical and mental health began to deteriorate. On the day of
her execution, she collapsed entirely and had to be transported to the
death chamber in a wheelchair. Subsequent reports suggested that she
was in a morphine-induced coma when the electricity flowed through
her body and ended her life.

With the smell of charred flesh still hanging in the air, Everett
Appelgate followed her to the chair, walking ramrod straight and
protesting his innocence to the end.

Jeffrey Daugherty

On Tuesday, March 2, 1976, three men driving to work at an asphalt plant near Melbourne, Florida, were stunned to see the body of a woman lying in a water-filled pit beside the road. The police were called and quickly determined that the woman had been shot in the head. Subsequent investigations identified the victim as Lavonne Patricia Sailer, a native of Tacoma, Washington. She'd last been seen hitchhiking outside of St. Cloud, Florida, where she'd gotten into an older model Ford Thunderbird.

With little more to go on, detectives focused their investigative efforts on tracking down the vehicle and soon had a hit from Alma, Michigan, where a similar car had been used in the armed robbery of a grocery store. The Pennsylvania State Police were also tracking the driver of a white Thunderbird and his female traveling companion. The couple had committed an armed robbery in Altoona and had been identified there as Jeffery Joseph Daugherty, 20, and his girlfriend, 41-year-old Bonnie Jean Heath. The couple also traveled intermittently with Raymond Daugherty Sr., Jeffery Daugherty's uncle.

Ray Daugherty had since parted company with the duo and once police picked him up he was able to fill in the details of a bloody road trip from Michigan to Florida during which Daugherty and Heath had committed countless robberies and at least five killings.

The first murder definitely attributed to Daugherty occurred on February 23, 1976, when he and Heath robbed a convenience store in Flagler Beach, Florida. The owners were both shot, the man taking four .22-caliber slugs to the head but somehow surviving. His wife was not so lucky. She died at the scene.

On March 1, 1976, Daugherty and Heath were driving through Brevard County when they picked up Lavonne Sailer. Sailer was robbed of her meager possessions and shot five times in the head. That same day, the deadly duo held up Betty's Pizza Parlor in Volusia County, beating and stabbing the proprietor, Betty Campbell, to death.

On March 4, with law enforcement agencies from several states now tracking them, the couple held up Ricche's Music Store in Altoona, Pennsylvania.

On the evening of March 9, they committed two more hold-ups in Altoona, shooting convenience store clerk, Elizabeth Shank, six times in the head. Two days later they gunned down 18-year-old George Karns while robbing a gas station.

Who knows how long Daugherty and Heath would have continued their murder spree had they not been caught. Fortunately, an alert Virginia state trooper spotted their vehicle on March 12 and gave chase, eventually taking the pair into custody. A search of their vehicle turned up a hunting knife and a couple of guns that were later matched by ballistics to the murder victims.

Now the various jurisdictions began lobbying to be the first to prosecute the pair. That honor fell to Virginia, who had, after all, captured the fugitives.

On July 1976, Daugherty was sentenced to 19 years in the Virginia State Penitentiary for crimes committed in that state. Murder convictions followed in Pennsylvania and in Volusia and Flagler Counties Florida, resulting in four life terms.

Brevard County authorities remained determined to seek the death penalty in the brutal slaying of Lavonne Sailer, shot down for a measly $12, all she owned in the world. Daugherty readily admitted to the murder but claimed that he'd been urged on by Bonnie Heath. It helped his case not in the least.

On April 27, 1981, Daugherty was sentenced to die in Florida's electric chair, a sentence eventually carried out on November 7, 1988. Bonnie Heath, meanwhile, was convicted on two counts of second-degree murder and sentenced to 25 years. By the time her accomplice was executed she had already been paroled.

Gregory Davis

Gregory Davis was born in Jackson, Mississippi, in 1966. The son of a Baptist minister, he grew up in a staunchly religious household. That notwithstanding, by the time he reached his teens, Davis had developed a dangerous sexual fixation with older women – not that anyone appreciated the seriousness of his obsession at the time, his exploits seemed innocent enough, if somewhat embarrassing to his family.

Davis's favorite pastime was hanging out at the local library, where he'd spend hours just staring at women. Sometimes he'd also wander the stacks and reach between the rows of books to fondle unsuspecting females. On other occasions, he'd deliberately drop a book on the floor, then try to peek up the skirts of women as they passed. Eventually, in January 1985, librarians called the police after a woman complained that Davis had tried to fondle her.

The charge was disorderly conduct, but additional charges were added when Davis was found to be in possession of stolen credit cards. Found guilty of a misdemeanor, he was packed off to attend a Job Corps program in Albany, Georgia. Here, he was soon up to his old tricks, wriggling under desks to fondle his female classmates' legs and on one occasion, exposing himself in the classroom. These actions could have got Davis in serious trouble, but unfortunately, Job Corps staff failed to report them. Their leniency would have tragic consequences.

On October 17, 1986, 59-year-old Lucy Spillers was strangled to death in her Albany home, just a block from the premises housing Job Corps trainees. She was found tied to her bed with a rope knotted tightly around her neck. She'd also been sexually mutilated with a butcher knife.

If Davis was suspected, he was never questioned. By November, he was back in Jackson, and on November 18, a murder startlingly similar to the Spillers homicide occurred there. Mary Dewitt, 81, was sexually assaulted and beaten to death in her home. Her body bore signs of post-mortem sexual mutilation.

Less than a month later, another elderly Jackson resident was murdered. Bertha Tanner was 83 when she died on December 11. She was raped, strangled, and sexually mutilated.

Three months would pass before the police had their first clue. On March 25, a 74-year-old Jackson woman was attacked in her home but survived. She was able to provide a description that would eventually lead police to Gregory Davis. Unfortunately, another elderly woman would die before an arrest was made.

On March 31, 1987, 80-year-old Addie Reid was attacked and killed. According to Davis's later confession, he'd gone to visit a friend on Manslip Street. Finding that his friend was not at home, he decided to burglarize the house next door, where Addie Reid lived alone.

He gained access through a bedroom window and stole $10 from Mrs. Reid's purse. Then he hid behind the bedroom door and waited for Reid to return. As the elderly woman entered the room she spotted

Davis and started to scream. Davis then struck her several times in the face, before dragging her into the dining room, where he strangled her to death. He had sex with the corpse before leaving.

On April 17, 1987, Davis was arrested on an unrelated burglary charge. Detectives, though, couldn't help noticing that he was a good match to the description provided by the survivor of the March 25 attack. They therefore began questioning him about the murders, and although he initially denied any involvement, Davis eventually broke down and confessed.

Gregory Davis would be tried for only one murder, that of Addie Reid. Found guilty, he was sentenced to death.

Donald Dufour

Over the course of the prior week, the postman working Henry Balch Drive, in Orlando Florida, had noticed that mail was piling up at one of the houses. That was no cause for alarm. People often went away and forgot to ask someone to clear their mail for them. It was only when the postman noticed a rancid odor coming from the house that he became concerned. On July 15, 1982, he passed those concerns on to the police.

A patrol unit was dispatched to the scene and forced the door. Inside, officers discovered the bodies of Ed Wise, aged 47, and John Stinson, 44. They appeared to have been shot and stabbed to death. The medical examiner concurred, adding that they'd been dead at least a week, possibly ten days. Further investigation revealed that the men were lovers, but had been devoted to each other, discounting the possibility that they might have picked up their killer at a bar and brought him home.

On September 6, a man riding his motorcycle through a citrus grove near Orlando was shocked at the sight of a corpse lying beside the road, partially covered by a blanket. The victim had been shot twice, .25-caliber bullets entering his head and back. A gasoline receipt, found in his pocket, identified him as Zack Miller. A scan of missing persons reports showed that his family had reported him missing two days previously.

When Miller's car was found the following day, police were hopeful of retrieving some evidence. But a month passed without progress and eventually the investigation, like that into the Wise / Stinson double homicide, became bogged down.

The break in the case came on October 10, when three hapless gunmen tried to hold up a local fast food restaurant. One of the men was captured near the scene and was quick to give up the "brains" of the outfit, a man who he named as Donald Dufour. Don was more than just a stick-up man, his captured accomplice said, he boasted of having killed over a dozen people, including a recent murder in an orange grove.

The mention of the orange grove murder caused the detectives' ears to prick up, but the would-be fast food bandit knew no more. Nonetheless, homicide investigators now had a name to work with and a concerted effort was launched to find Dufour. Four days later, he was tracked to Jackson, Mississippi. Unfortunately, Mississippi was not prepared to consider an extradition order. Dufour had just been charged there with a double homicide.

Gay lovers, Danny King, 32, and Earl Peeples, 34, had been found stabbed to death in Peeples' apartment. Forensic evidence tied Dufour to the scene. Despite his protestations of innocence, he was found guilty and sentenced to die in Mississippi's electric chair.

Dufour was subsequently returned to Florida where he pled guilty to killing Ed Wise in exchange for a life sentence. The Stinson murder charge was dropped altogether, but Dufour wasn't so lucky in the Miller case. The guilty verdict earned him another death penalty.

Donald Dufour was returned to Mississippi to await execution. Should that sentence ever be commuted, he will still face the death penalty in Florida.

Gary Charles Evans

From an early age, Gary Evans showed many of the classic signs of antisocial personality disorder. Physically and emotionally abused as a child, he grew up to be a compulsive liar, a habitual thief and an abuser of pets and other small animals. He also developed pre-pubescent drug and alcohol habits and by his teens he was living on the streets, making his way by stealing from local drug dealers. He earned his first jail time in 1970, for breaking and entering. Thereafter, he accumulated a lengthy rap sheet for petty thievery.

By the mid-1970s, Evans had set his goals higher. Having acquired a great deal of book knowledge on antiques, he set himself up as a burglar of high-end merchandise, bringing in two childhood friends, Michael Falco and Timothy Rysedorph, as accomplices.

At first, the partnership worked well. Evans would case out potential targets by posing as an antiques dealer and talking to store owners. He'd then return at night with Falco and Rysedorph to rob the place.

Eventually, his luck ran out, earning him a stretch in Clinton Correctional Facility. Paroled in March 1980, he was soon back in jail for possession of stolen property. Thereafter, he was in and out of jail until the mid-eighties.

In February 1985, shortly after his release from his latest period of incarceration, Evans committed his first murder, killing accomplice Michael Falco with a bullet to the head. Evans told local hoods and the police that Falco had fled to California. In truth, Falco was wrapped in a sleeping bag, sunk to the bottom of a swamp near Lake Worth, Florida.

On April 21, 1985, Evans was involved in a high-speed chase with police officers following a $12,000 heist. That led to a 2-to-4 year stretch in Sing Sing, where he befriended David Berkowitz, the notorious "Son of Sam."

Back on the streets in March 1988, Evans began working with a new accomplice,

Damien Cuomo. On September 8, the pair robbed a jewelry store in Watertown, New York, during which Evans shot and killed the proprietor, 63-year-old Douglas J. Berry. Afraid that Cuomo would turn him in for the murder, Evans took care of business on December 27, 1989, shooting Cuomo in the head and burying his body. He then moved in with Cuomo's girlfriend.

On October 17, 1991, Evans shot and killed jewelry shop owner Gregory Jouben, 36, in Herkimer County, New York. The murder would remain unsolved until Evans confessed to it.

Evans was back in prison in 1993, securing an early release by striking a deal to coax a jailhouse confession out of a fellow inmate. The man was eventually charged with one murder. Evans, who had snitched on him, had already committed four.

In October 1997, that body count was increased by one when Evans shot and killed long-term associate Timothy Rysedorph. He then dismembered Rysedorph's body with a chainsaw before disposing of it.

Rysedorph's sudden disappearance coincided with Evan's skipping out on his probation, which immediately aroused police suspicions. They were certain that Rysedorph was dead and that Evans was in hiding. A nationwide manhunt was launched, lasting eight months before Evans was eventually caught near St. Johnsbury, Vermont. He'd been living in a tent in the woods.

Despite finally running their quarry to ground, the police actually had very little on Evans. He would likely have walked, had he not inexplicably confessed to the five murders he'd committed. He later assisted police in recovering the bodies of Falco, Cuomo and Rysedorph.

Evans was indicted for murder in Rensselaer County, New York, on August 12, 1998. While being transported to an Albany court, Evans managed to free his hands, kick out a side window, and jump from the vehicle.

Cornered by police, he jumped from the bridge to his death in the shallows of the Hudson River, 60 feet below.

Christine Falling

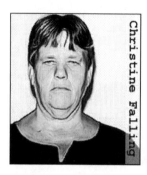

Christine Falling was born in Perry, Florida, on March 12, 1963. Like most serial killers, she did not have the best start in life. Her mother, Ann, was just 16 when Christine was born and had already given birth to another child. Her father, Thomas Slaughter, was 65-years-old, a violent, abusive man whose meager wages ensured that his family lived in extreme poverty.

Falling grew up developmentally disabled, her comprehension and vocabulary skills never advancing beyond those of a sixth-grader. She was prone to obesity, suffered fits of epilepsy and was quick to resort to aggressive behavior.

Partly because of this, and partly because they were unable to support their daughters, Christine's parents put them up for adoption. The girls were taken in by the Falling family, who soon learned that Christine and her sister were impossible to control.

Unable to cope, the Fallings placed the siblings in a children's home, where Christine would remain until the age of 12. It was during this time that she first began directing her violent tendencies towards animals, a trait common to many serial killers.

After leaving the home, Falling tracked her birth mother to Blountstown, Florida, and moved there to live with her. Two years later, at the age of just fourteen, she married a man in his twenties. The marriage was marred by violence and soon fell apart, whereupon Falling developed symptoms that suggested Munchausen Syndrome. She began visiting local hospitals complaining of a catalog of ailments, from vaginal bleeding to snakebite. These always turned out to be false.

Around this time, Falling began taking on babysitting jobs. Despite her disheveled appearance and obvious mental difficulties, she gained a reputation as someone who was reliable and who loved children. What the trusting parents didn't know was that Falling was covertly hurting their children. Soon, she'd go way beyond that.

On February 28, 1980, Cassidy Johnson, a two-year-old girl who Falling had been babysitting, died from what was assumed to be encephalitis. An autopsy was performed and showed that the child had, in fact, suffered a severe skull injury. Falling was pulled in for questioning but insisted that the baby had fallen from her crib. The police didn't believe her but were unable to prove otherwise.

Falling next moved to Lakeland, Florida, where she soon killed another toddler. Four-year-old Jeffrey Davis had shown no prior signs of illness when (according to Falling) he suddenly stopped breathing.

An autopsy was performed but could not conclusively determine cause of death.

Three days later, Falling was asked to babysit Jeffrey's cousin, two-year-old Joseph Spring, while his parents attended Jeffrey's funeral. Joseph inexplicably died while taking a nap, his death attributed to a viral infection which doctors now believed may also have killed Jeffrey.

Shortly after Joseph Spring's death, Falling moved to her hometown of Perry, Florida, where she found work as a housekeeper to 77-year-old Wilbur Swindle. On Falling's first day at this job, Swindle suddenly collapsed and died in his kitchen. Due to his old age and deteriorating health, no suspicions were raised.

Soon after Swindle's death, Falling's eighteen-month-old niece, Jennifer Daniels, allegedly stopped breathing while under Falling's care. This time too, the death was ruled to be from natural causes and Falling did not come under suspicion.

A year would pass before Falling claimed her next victim. On July 2, 1982, ten-week-old Travis Coleman stopped breathing while Falling was attending to him. An autopsy was ordered and revealed that the baby had been suffocated.

Falling was brought in for questioning and admitted to killing three babies by what she called "smotheration." She'd press a blanket over their faces, she said, holding it there until they were still. Asked why she'd done it, she said that she heard voices instructing her to kill.

Falling was found guilty of murder and sentenced to life imprisonment, with eligibility for parole after 25 years.

Joseph J. Fischer

Joseph Fischer was born in Belleville, New Jersey in 1923. His father
was a construction worker, his mother a prostitute who brought her
tricks home while her husband was at work. What impact this had on
Fischer's subsequent crime spree is unknown, although he later
confessed a deep-seated hatred for his mother. "I would have killed her
10 times over," he said, "but I really believed that it would have
broken my father's heart."

Enrolled in Catholic school, Fischer was an unruly student who took to
criminality from an early age. Eventually, it landed him in a
reformatory.

Released in 1938, Fischer lied about his age to join the merchant
marine. But he soon went AWOL and returned to New Jersey. In
1941, he enlisted in the Marine Corps and saw action at Guadalcanal,
Kwajalein, and Iwo Jima. Later, he was posted to mainland China to
guard military trains While thus engaged he shot and killed a number
of Chinese civilians. He avoided being court marshaled by insisting
the civilians were bandits intent on robbing the military transports.
Nonetheless, he was diagnosed a dangerous paranoid schizophrenic
and discharged from the service in 1945.

Fischer found it difficult to adapt to civilian life and soon ran foul of
the law. He was arrested on numerous occasions and did time in
various mental institutions. Eventually, in 1948, he was sent down for

robbery and assault. Paroled in December 1953, he was free only a matter of days before he attacked a 16-year-old boy and beat him to death with a rock. That crime earned him a 25-year prison term.

While in prison, Fischer began corresponding with a wealthy widow named Claudine Eggers. Upon his release in June 1978, Fischer married his 78-year-old sweetheart, the main attraction being her money. Over the next 13 months, the odd couple traveled the country, with Claudine picking up the bill.

On July 2, 1979, Fischer walked into a police station in Wassaic, New York, and confessed to killing his wife. Officers responding to the information found Claudine at the couple's home, stabbed to death.

Fischer was charged with second-degree murder, but he wasn't done yet. As investigators sat gape-mouthed he began a rambling confession, admitting to another 18 homicides in a cross-country spree.

Initially skeptical of his claims, the police began checking and discovered that Fischer was wanted in Arizona and Oklahoma for a couple of murders committed there. Fischer also claimed to have killed in Los Angeles; San Francisco; New Mexico; Cooperstown, New York; Hartford, Connecticut; and Portland, Maine.

A photo found in his possession was of a murder victim from Ruidos, New Mexico, named Pamela Nolen. Police also found evidence that linked Fischer to the beating death of a man in Flagstaff, Arizona, and to the stabbing of two 17-year-old girls in Norwalk, Connecticut.

Despite this evidence, Fischer was charged only with the murder of his wife. He went on trial in April 1980 and was found guilty. The sentence was 25 years to life. Warrants remained outstanding in several other jurisdictions but none of them were inclined to extradite, thus robbing Fischer of the chance at infamy he so obviously craved.

He compensated by making pronouncements from his cell at Sing Sing, his self-proclaimed victim count growing eventually to 150. Appearances on "Geraldo," "A Current Affair," and "America's Most Wanted," garnered him some attention, but by the time he died in 1991, Joe Fischer's death caused barely a ripple. His true body count will never be known.

Alfred Gaynor

"I know it's hard to understand but I truly am a good person." Thus spoke Alfred J. Gaynor, confessed murderer of eight women and a 22-month-old baby. The occasion for this outpouring was a November 2010 court appearance where Gaynor, already serving life without parole for four murders, addressed the families of three more of his victims.

"All I have left to give is the truth," he said magnanimously as he described the murders of Jill Ann Ermellini, 34; Robin Atkins, 29; and Yvette Torres, 33.

Jill Ermellini's badly decomposed body had been discovered inside the cab of an abandoned truck on June 16, 1997. According to Gaynor, he'd lured her there with the promise of smoking some crack. When she discovered he didn't have any, she tried to leave but Gaynor prevented her from doing so. Grabbing her by the throat, he insisted on sex. When she refused, he choked her into unconsciousness, raped her, and then strangled her to death.

Gaynor's next victim was Robin Atkins, found strangled, bound and gagged in an alleyway on October 25, 1997. She was naked except for one sock, the other knotted around her neck in a ligature. Her hands were tied behind her back with a bootlace. Gaynor's M.O. in this murder was similar to that in the previous one. He lured Atkins into the alley with the promise of smoking crack, then overpowered and raped her before strangling her to death. Later, he took the change from her purse to pay for bus fare home.

Less than a month later, on November 15, 1997, Yvette Torres' 11-year-old son came home to find his mother's partially clothed corpse propped up against the bathroom door at her apartment. Gaynor said that he raped and strangled Torres before stealing her video recorder and selling it to buy drugs.

Gaynor also confessed to killing 45-year-old Vera E. Hallums on April 20, 1995. Hallums was his first victim, he said, preceding the four murders that had earned him his life sentence. She'd been found tied, beaten and strangled to death in her apartment.

The most depraved of Gaynor's evil deeds, though, was the July 1996 murder of 20-year-old Amy Smith and her 22-month-old daughter, Destiny.

On the day in question, Gaynor arrived at Smith's apartment with his nephew Paul Fickling. Smith was Fickling's ex-girlfriend and he believed that he was the father of her child (tests would later prove that this wasn't the case). Shortly after they arrived, Fickling and Smith got into and argument, whereupon he punched the woman and put her in a headlock. Gaynor then shoved a sock into Amy's mouth and bound her hands. He then told Fickling to leave.

No one but Gaynor knows what happened next. According to Gaynor, he raped Smith before strangling her and pushing her into a closet, still bound and gagged. He then fled the apartment, leaving the baby alone with her mother's corpse. Amy Smith's body and that of her baby were found a week later. Amy had died of asphyxiation, the toddler of starvation and dehydration.

Alfred Gaynor was handed additional life terms for the murders he'd confessed to. Not that it mattered; he was never getting out of prison anyway. Based upon Gaynor's confession to the Smith double homicide, Paul Fickling's life term was reduced to 20 years.

Ronald Gray

Born in Cochran, Georgia in 1966, Ronald Gray grew up in Miami, Florida. His childhood was characterized by poverty and abuse and he escaped at the first opportunity, joining the U.S. Army in 1984, at age 18. Gray trained as a cook and in 1986 was posted to Fort Bragg, outside Fayetteville, North Carolina. Shortly after his arrival, the base and the nearby town experienced a rash of brutal murders.

The first occurred on April 29, 1986, when 24-year-old Private Linda Coats was found dead in her trailer at Fayetteville. She'd been raped and shot in the head.

A few days later, soldiers at Fort Bragg found the naked, battered corpse of Fayetteville prostitute, Teresa Utley. Recently reported missing, Utley had been raped and sodomized, then beaten and stabbed to death.

After the Utley murder, the killer went to ground, emerging again on November 16, when he abducted and raped two Fayetteville women at gunpoint. Threatened with their lives if they reported the incident, the women kept it to themselves.

Another Fayetteville woman was attacked on November 22, raped, stabbed, and left for dead. That same night a female soldier was attacked on the Fort Bragg reservation. She, too, survived.

On December 12, the 18-year-old wife of a Fort Bragg soldier was abducted from her home in Bonnie Doone. Tammy Wilson's naked body was discovered in nearby woods, hours later. She had been raped and shot at point-blank range.

Just three days later, the Fort Bragg killer claimed another victim. Sgt. Michael Clay was away on maneuvers when he received word that his mobile home in Fayetteville had burned to the ground. His wife, Private Laura Clay, was missing from the scene. Her body would be found five weeks later in some woods nearby.

Before that happened, another female soldier was attacked. She survived, but Fayetteville cab driver Kimberly Ruggles was not so lucky. Reported missing on January 7, Ruggles' cab was found abandoned on a street in Fayetteville. Her body turned up a day later on the Fort Bragg reservation. She'd been raped, sodomized, and beaten. Death was caused by a knife wound that had hacked through the main veins and arteries in her throat.

With this latest murder, the two surviving rape victims eventually mustered the courage to go to the police. Since the attack, one of the victims had spotted her assailant on the street and followed him to his home. She now shared that information with the police.

Ronald Gray was placed under immediate surveillance and eventually indicted   by the civilian authorities on 23 felony charges, including first-degree murder, first-degree rape, kidnapping, burglary, and armed robbery.

On November 5, 1987, Gray pled guilty to all charges in a Fayetteville courtroom. He was sentenced to three consecutive terms of life imprisonment. However, the law wasn't done with Ronald Gray just yet. He still had to face a court-martial for the crimes committed on the Fort Bragg military base.

Those proceedings began in December 1987 and concluded on April 12, 1988, with a unanimous guilty verdict. Gray was sentenced to death, the sentence (as required by law) later affirmed by US president George W. Bush.

Ronald Gray currently awaits execution at the Federal Correctional Complex in Terre Haute, Indiana.

Douglas Gretzler & William Steelman

In late December of 1972, 22-year-old Douglas Gretzler abandoned his wife and infant daughter in New York City and headed west. After drifting for a while, he ended up in Denver, Colorado, where he met William Steelman.

Steelman, 28 at the time of that fateful meeting, already had a lengthy rap sheet. He'd also been jailed for forgery and had spent time in a mental institution. Perhaps noticing a kindred spirit, one in the other, the two men hit it off immediately. They began traveling the country together. Soon they'd unleash an unprecedented orgy of bloodshed.

The spree that would catapult Gretzler and Steelman to infamy began on October 17, 1973, when they murdered Ken Unrein and Mike Adshade, acquaintances of Steelman, and stole their camper van. They next decided to drive to Mesa, Arizona, to visit 19-year-old Bob Robbins and his 18-year-old girlfriend Yafah Hacohen, who Steelman knew. On route, they picked up a hitcher, Steve Loughren, later killing him and leaving his body in the Superstition Desert.

Arriving in Mesa they went to the trailer home where Robbins and Hacohen lived. Hacohen was at work when they arrived, so they killed Robbins, and then waited for Hacohen to return. She was stabbed and garroted to death.

The killers next headed for Tucson and managed to thumb a ride with 19-year-old Gilbert Sierra. For his kindness, Sierra got a bullet in the head and ended up dumped in the desert. The deadly pair then drove Sierra's car to Tucson, abandoning it at a parking garage.

On November 3, they kidnapped Vincent Armstrong after he stopped to give them a ride. Fortunately, Armstrong managed to escape and gave police a description of his abductors. An APB was quickly issued but it arrived too late to save newlyweds, Michael and Patricia Sandberg. After forcing their way into the Sandberg's home, Gretzler and Steelman executed the young couple before ransacking their apartment and driving away in their car.

With a warrant now out for their arrest, Gretzler and Steelman headed west. On November 6, they arrived in the tiny hamlet of Victor, California, 40 miles south of Sacramento.

Walter and Joanne Parkin had gone bowling that night, leaving their children –Lisa, 11, and Robert, 9 – in the care of 18-year-old neighbor Debra Earl. During the course of the evening, Debra's parents dropped by, along with her fiancée, Mark Lang, and her brother Richard. When the Parkins returned home, they found their friends and neighbors being held at gunpoint by two men. They too were taken captive.

At around 3 a.m., Carol Jenkins, a houseguest of the Parkins, returned from a date and went straight to bed. She was roused near dawn by two friends of Mark Lang, who had spent the night looking for him after he failed to return home. Jenkins said that she hadn't seen him, but went to wake Walter and Joanne Parkin to see if they knew anything. She found them in the master bedroom. Both had been shot in the head.

The police were called, arriving soon after to find seven more bodies, including those of the two children, crammed into a walk-in closet. All of the victims were bound and gagged, each had been shot in the head, execution style. Twenty-five bullets would later be removed from the nine bodies.

A massive manhunt was launched and eventually tracked Gretzler and Steelman to a Sacramento hotel. They were arrested on November 8, surrendering without a fight.

Under interrogation, Gretzler cracked almost immediately, confessing to the Parkin massacre and also to the series of homicides in Arizona. In June 1974, Gretzler and Steelman were convicted in California on nine counts of murder and sentenced to life in prison without parole.

But the law wasn't done with the loathsome duo yet. Extradited to Arizona they were tried and found guilty of killing Michael and Patricia Sandberg. The penalty, this time, was death.

That sentence would never be carried out on William Steelman. He died of liver disease after spending 10 years on death row. Gretzler, however, would keep his date with the executioner. His appeals exhausted, he was eventually put to death by lethal injection in 1988.

Alejandro Henriquez

At first, the NYPD was reluctant to admit that a serial killer was stalking the children of the South Bronx. The fact that all of the victims were Hispanic and had lived within two miles of each other, the fact that their brutalized bodies had been dumped in various parks in the area, was purely coincidental, they said. The discrepancies between the crimes outweighed the similarities.

Eventually, though, faced with an angry and frustrated community, they were forced to admit that a single perpetrator might be responsible. Belatedly they put together a task force to investigate the murders. By then, four children and a young woman were dead.

The first victim was a 14-year-old girl named Shamira Bello. Shamira had gone missing from the neighborhood on July 2, 1988. She'd been discovered in Pelham Bay Park a few days later, sexually assaulted and bludgeoned to death.

A year went by, during which the police made very little progress on the case. Then, in June 1989, two more children were gone. Nilda Cartagena, 13, and Heriberto Marrero, 15, were found near the Whitestone Bridge on June 21, 1989. Both had been strangled.

Almost a year to the day later, on June 14, 1990, 21-year-old Lisa Ann Rodriguez was found raped and strangled along the Hutchinson River Parkway. Three months later, 10-year-old Jessica Guzman vanished. Her brutalized corpse turned up near the Bronx River Parkway.

This latest murder served as a rallying cry for the community. More than 2,000 turned up at Jessica's funeral, they held vigils, rallies, and press conferences, they raised money to fund additional police patrols, they put pressure on the NYPD via the media. Eventually, the police relented and assigned 40 officers to a dedicated task force.

There was little physical evidence to go on, but as investigators started questioning friends and relatives of the victims a strong circumstantial case began to emerge. One man was linked to all of the victims. He had known Shamira Bello; he was Nilda Cartagena's uncle; he had dated Lisa Ann Rodriguez; he was dating a woman whose daughter was Jessica Guzman's best friend and he was one of the last people seen with Jessica before she disappeared.

His name was Alejandro Henriquez, a 31-year-old livery cab operator who lived in the area and had participated in the search for Jessica Guzman and the subsequent candlelight prayer vigils for the victims.

Henriquez was brought in for questioning and although he was cooperative, the answers he gave to some of the questions aroused police suspicions. For example, he initially denied knowing Lisa Ann Rodriguez, only admitting that he'd dated her when the police said they had witnesses who could back it up.

There was physical evidence too, three strands of hair found on Shamira Bello's body were positively matched to Henriquez, and fibers found in a vacuum cleaner in Henriquez's apartment had come from three of the victims.

Even more damaging were Henriquez's attempts to deflect attention from himself. First, he paid a young friend to follow the police around as they scoured the dumpsites looking for clues. Then he tried to convince his nephew to make calls to the media pretending to be the killer. In doing so he slipped up and told the nephew details of the crimes that only the killer would know.

Henriquez went on trial in 1992, charged with the murders of Jessica Guzman, Lisa Ann Rodriguez, and Shamira Bello. Despite his protestations of innocence, he was found guilty and sentenced to 25 years to life on each count. That means he will have to serve a minimum of 75 years before becoming eligible for parole.

Henriquez has never been charged with the Cartagena and Marrero murders, although he remains the prime suspect in those cases.

Monroe Hickson

A native of South Carolina, born in 1909, Monroe Hickson first came to the attention of police in 1931, when he was convicted of assault with intent to kill. That earned him a five-year prison term. He served only two before being paroled in 1933.

Following his release, he stayed out of trouble for almost a decade before landing himself back in prison in 1942, this time for petty larceny. Five years later, he was arrested after an armed robbery in New Holland, South Carolina, and sentenced to 20 years. With time off for good behavior, he was out by April 1957.

Just months after his release, on August 7, Hickson entered a dry goods store in Graniteville, South Carolina, assaulted the owner Lucy Parker, and escaped with a small amount of cash from the register. Arrested on August 8, it looked like he was destined for yet another short jail term. But after nine days in the jailhouse, Hickson astounded his captors by confessing to a series of brutal killings, committed between April and September 1946.

The first murder occurred on April 17, 1946, when Hickson entered a grocery store in Aiken, South Carolina, bludgeoned the owner, David Garrett, to death with an ax, and escaped with $22 in cash. The robbery also netted him a pistol, which he used eleven days later, in another robbery. Mr. and Mrs. Edward Bennett were shot to death at their place of business, the killer making off with a paltry $8, plus another pistol. Hickson was questioned in connection with the crime but was released due to lack of evidence.

With shopkeepers now on high alert in the small town, Hickson changed his M.O. On September 28, 1946, he invaded the home of Annie Wiseberg in Aiken, beating her to death with a length of stove wood and making off with $5. On December 4, he reverted to type, holding up a liquor store and beating the clerk, Christine Cholakis, with a brick. Cholakis survived the attack but was unable to provide a description of her attacker, other than to say that he was a black man.

The police, meanwhile, had arrested a man named L.D. Harris for the Bennett murders. Harris was tried and sentenced to death, the penalty later reduced to life in prison, on appeal. He remained locked up until Hickson's confession finally cleared him in 1957.

Hickson eventually stood trial on four counts of first-degree murder. Found guilty, he was sentenced to life plus twenty years. On March 10, 1966, he escaped from the state prison in Columbia, South Carolina. Despite a massive effort, which included his name being listed on the FBI's Most Wanted list, he was never recaptured.

Neither did he spend very long as a fugitive. In December 1967, while hiding out in New Bern, North Carolina, under the alias Willie Tyler, Hickson fell ill. He was admitted to the New Bern hospital and later transferred to Chapel Hill, where he died of natural causes on December 29. Federal agents traced him there a year later and identified his remains from fingerprints.

Anthony Jackson

Eight years after Bostonians breathed a collective sigh of relief at the conclusion of the Boston Strangler case, another deadly psychopath began menacing the women of the city. Unlike the Strangler, the Hitchhiker Killer, as he'd become known, was particular about the type of victim he targeted. He preferred pretty college age women, and if they made it easier for him by thumbing rides, well that was all to the good.

The killer first announced himself to the world late in September 1972. Kathleen Randall, 18 years old and newly enrolled at Boston University was last seen near the campus, standing at the side of the road and trying to hitch a ride. Her brutalized corpse turned up in rural New Hampshire, two weeks later. She'd been raped and strangled.

Two days after Kate Randall disappeared another young woman was attacked, this one in Lynn, Massachusetts. Nineteen-year-old Debra Stevens was found lying by the side of the road, just 50 yards from her home. Her killer had throttled her to death before carelessly discarding her remains. Like Kathleen Randall, she had been raped.

Victim number three was Ellen Reich, a 19-year-old sophomore at Emerson College, and a habitual hitchhiker. Ellen lived off campus in the Back Bay area and traveled to and from her classes by thumbing rides. That habit cost her life on November 9. This time, though, the killer made some effort to conceal the body. She was found four days later on November 14, hanging inside a closet in an abandoned house in Roxbury. Cause of death was determined to be strangulation, although she'd also been stabbed several times.

Sandra Ehramjian, 21, was a part-time Boston taxi driver who, ironically, didn't own a car. When not driving her cab she made her way around by hitchhiking. A resident of Cambridge, Sandra was on her way to a dentist's appointment when she vanished on November 27. Her body was found the next day, dumped in a culvert near Waldo Lake, in Brockton.

Two days later, another young woman, 22-year-old honor student Synge Gillespie, set out to hitch a ride and promptly disappeared. After her parents appealed for help via the media, they received a call from a man demanding a $25,000 ransom. It was a hoax, of course. Synge was already dead. Her decomposed corpse would eventually be found on February 3, 1973, in a heavily wooded area near Billerica. By then, a suspect would be in custody.

The police got their break in the case on the evening of December 26, 1972. At around 8 p.m. two Cambridge patrolmen observed a man trying to talk a woman into his gold-colored Cadillac. The officers approached the man who drove off at high speed. Soon after, they found the car, now standing empty, and saw the man walking nearby. As they approached, he drew a gun and started firing. A brief gunfight ensued during which the man ran off. He was found a short distance away, lying on the ground, having been struck by a bullet.

The shooter was 33-year-old Anthony Jackson and he was booked for attempted murder, assault with a deadly weapon, and illegal possession of a firearm. However, when officers searched his car, they found traces of blood. Subsequent inquiries linked him to the disappearance of Synge Gillespie, and he was charged with her murder on February 3, 1973, the day her body was found. Physical evidence and the testimony of several acquaintances later linked him to the other murders.

Jackson was tried and found guilty on five counts of first-degree murder. He was sentenced to life in prison without parole. The "Hitchhiker Murders" stopped abruptly after his arrest.

Edwin Kaprat III

Someone was killing the elderly citizens of Brooksville, causing panic in the quiet retirement community 60 miles north of Tampa, Florida. The first to die had been 80-year-old Sophia Garrity, raped and beaten to death in her home on August 7, 1993. Her house had then been set on fire to conceal the crime, leading investigators to believe that she had died in a fire caused by an electrical short.

A similar diagnosis was offered when 70-year-old Ruth Goldsmith's burned body was found at her mobile home the following day. But by the time 79-year-old Lydia Ridell died on September 2, the sudden rash of fires seemed like too much of a coincidence. The police began to suspect that a serial killer might be at work, an opinion firmed up when Sophia Garrity's 87-year-old neighbor, Loraine Dawe, died on September 29.

In addition to the murders, an elderly couple, William and Alice Whitney, had been attacked and severely beaten in their home on

August 17. Their attacker had then set the house on fire. The Whitleys would likely have died, but for a quick-thinking neighbor's response to their smoke alarm.

With the community in uproar and many elderly residents moving in with family or leaving town, police got their first break in the case. The day after the Dawe murder, an anonymous caller contacted the Hernando County Sheriff's Office and suggested that the police take a closer look at Edwin Kaprat, recently arrived in town and living with his sister.

Taking the caller's advice, police looked into Kaprat's past and turned up some interesting information. Kaprat had been arrested two years earlier, for robbing and murdering a man on a Tampa highway. He'd walked on the murder rap due to lack of evidence, but had served a period of house arrest for using the dead man's credit cards. The police also found out that Kaprat knew all of the Brooksville victims, having worked at each of their homes as a handyman.

It was compelling, but hardly enough to make a murder conviction. They therefore placed the hulking 29-year-old under surveillance, while they firmed up their case.

Kaprat was taken into custody on October 8, charged with four counts of murder and two of attempted murder. He made no pretense at innocence, describing in sickening detail the attacks on his frail victims. Of the Dawe murder, the 200-pound killer said that he, "stepped on her neck and broke it to put her out of her misery" because she was having a heart attack while he was sexually assaulting her. Asked why he'd committed the murders Kaprat said that he had urges he couldn't control.

Kaprat went on trial in early 1995. Despite his earlier confessions, he entered "not guilty" pleas to the 18 felony charges against him. It did him no good. Given the death penalty on February 28, 1995, he lasted just six weeks in prison. On April 19, 1995, fellow inmates Mario Lara and Rigoberto Sanchez-Velasco knifed him to death.

Posteal Laskey

Between October 1965 and December 1966, a brutal strangler terrorized the city of Cincinnati, Ohio. The killer targeted mainly older women, raping and throttling them in a series of crimes frighteningly reminiscent of the recent "Boston Strangler" murders in Massachusetts. Seven women died and one was injured before the arrest of a suspect brought the reign of terror to an abrupt halt. By then, the press had coined a sobriquet for the phantom murderer. They called him the "Cincinnati Strangler."

The killer first announced his presence on October 12, 1965, when he beat and raped a 65-year-old woman, then knotted a length of clothesline around her neck and attempted to strangle her. Fortunately, she survived.

The next victim, Emogene Harrington, was not so lucky. She was found in the basement of her apartment building on December 2, strangled to death.

On April 4, 1966, the strangler killed again, throttling 58-year-old Lois Dant to death in her first-floor Cincinnati apartment. Two months later, on June 10, he was back. Jeannette Messer, age 56, was found in a city park, raped and strangled with a necktie.

The word was now out. A killer was on the loose in the city, and as panic descended there was a run on locks, security systems, firearms, and ammunition. It did nothing to discourage the strangler.

On October 12, 51-year-old Carol Hochhausler was found beaten, raped, and throttled to death in the garage of her home. Eight days later, 81-year-old Rose Winstsel was beaten and sexually assaulted before being strangled with a length of electrical cord.

The police were no closer to tracking down the killer when another octogenarian, Lula Kerrick, was found strangled to death in the elevator of her apartment building on December 9.

On August 14, Cincinnati police received a report of a car accident in the Price Hill area of the city. Patrolman Frank Sefton responded to the call, but as he approached the scene at the corner of Ring Place and Grand Avenue, he could see right away that this was no accident. A Yellow Cab stood in the middle of the rain-soaked intersection. Nearby on the pavement lay a woman, her clothing askew, her right foot almost severed, her throat cut and bleeding profusely.

Further investigation revealed that the woman was Barbara Bowman, a 31-year-old secretary who worked nearby. An eyewitness reported that Ms. Bowman had been involved in a tussle with the cabbie and had jumped from the cab with blood flowing from her neck. As she'd tried to flee, the cab had run her down and the driver, described as a slim, black man, had abandoned the vehicle and fled on foot. A check with the cab company revealed that the cab had been stolen earlier that day.

On December 8, a man tried to force his way into an apartment on West Court Street. Frustrated in his efforts, he left, but not before an eyewitness wrote down his license plate number. The number was passed on to police, who arrested ex-con Posteal Laskey the following day.

They immediately noted his resemblance to the man seen fleeing the Bowman murder scene. Then, after learning that Laskey had previously worked for the cab company, and finding a master key in his possession, he was charged with murder.

Laskey stood trial for the murder of Barbara Bowman in 1967. Found guilty, he was sentenced to death, the sentence commuted to life imprisonment when the Supreme Court outlawed capital punishment in 1972. He died in prison on May 29, 2007.

Although, he was never charged in the Cincinnati Strangler murders, the investigative team was certain that he was the man responsible. They consider it no coincidence that the murders abruptly stopped after his arrest.

Diana Lumbrera

In 1974, a pregnant 17-year-old, named Diana Lumbrera, married her boyfriend Lionel Garza in Bovina, Texas. The following year, she bore him a healthy daughter who the couple named Melissa. Another daughter followed the next year, named Joanna, but by now the marriage was already in trouble, marred by constant fighting between Diana and Lionel. Then, when Joanna was just three months old, tragedy struck. While the baby was alone with Diana, she started experiencing convulsions. By the time Diana got her to the hospital, she was already dead. Joanna's death was blamed on asphyxiation due to convulsive disorder, an unavoidable tragedy.

There was happier news for the Garza family soon after. Diana was pregnant again and in 1977 gave birth to a son, Jose Lionel.

On February 10, 1978, Diana rushed the two-month-old Jose to the emergency room. The baby had suddenly gone into convulsions and stopped breathing, she said. Fortunately, doctors were able to resuscitate him and thereafter placed him in the pediatric intensive care unit. He seemed to be doing well, but that afternoon Diana phoned her husband to tell him that Jose was dying.

At around 6:30 that evening, a nurse saw Diana run from the baby's room in tears. She checked immediately on the child and found him unconscious. Thirty minutes later, despite the best efforts of doctors, Jose was dead.

Less than eight months later, on October 2, Diana walked into the Bovina emergency room with daughter Melissa dead in her arms. She told her familiar tale of unexplained convulsions followed by rapid death. Amazingly, despite her history, medical staff believed her. Melissa's death was put down to natural causes and no autopsy was called for.

The strain of this latest death finally pushed the Garza's teetering marriage over the edge. They were divorced in 1979. Diana never remarried but over the next seven years, she'd give birth to three more children, each with a different father. All of them would fall victim to what Diana now referred to as a curse.

But it was not only her own children who were at risk. On October 8, 1980, Diana was caring for six-week-old Ericka Aleman, the daughter of a cousin. While under Diana's supervision, the child suddenly stopped breathing. Diana rushed her to the emergency room where she was pronounced dead on arrival.

There was yet another tragedy on August 17, 1982. Diana's two-year-old daughter, Melinda, her first child born out of wedlock, died at home, cause of death listed as acute heart failure. Fifteen months later, Diana bore another son, named Daniel. He died on March 25, 1984, apparently from septicemia. If physicians suspected foul play, they kept it to themselves.

In 1985, Diana moved to Garden City, Kansas. Within a year of settling there, she gave birth to another son, Jose Antonio, born on February 21, 1986.

Jose Antonio survived longer than any of his siblings. He was four years and three months old when, on May 1, 1990, his mother carried his tiny corpse into a hospital emergency room. This time, though, hospital staff did not buy Diana's convulsion story. The police were called and she found herself under arrest.

The arrest sparked the authorities in Texas into action. New investigations were launched and it was discovered that each of the Lumbrera children had been insured, for amounts ranging from $3,000 to $5,000. With motive established, charges were brought in the deaths of each of the children. Lumbrera received a life sentence in Kansas and was then extradited to Texas to face murder charges there.

The Texas charges carried the possibility of the death penalty, leading to Lumbrera striking a deal for life imprisonment. She pled guilty to Melissa's murder, while charges were dropped in the cases of Melinda and Joanna. She then entered a plea of "no contest" to the charge of murdering Jose Lionel, adding another life sentence to her time.

Diana Lumbrera is currently incarcerated in Kansas. If she ever earns parole from that sentence she will be extradited to Texas, to serve her time there.

Frank Masini

If the road to hell is paved with good intentions, then the road to serial homicide is paved with telltale predictors, small acts of cruelty and petty criminality that eventually escalate to murder. Serial killers most often have troubled childhoods, display one or more of a triad of juvenile behaviors (bed-wetting, animal cruelty and pyromania) and commit various petty thefts and sexual offenses before they graduate to killing.

That accounts for most cases. But in a small, though not insignificant portion, there is no indication of the monster that lurks beneath the outwardly normal façade.

One such case involved Frank Masini, a 48-year-old carpenter from Livingston, New Jersey. Masini, who had emigrated from Italy at the age of 17, was an apparently happily married man with two children. He ran his own carpentry business and had no history of criminality or of drug or alcohol abuse. He was, in the words of the defense attorney at his trial, "living the American dream."

Yet over a two-week period in 1991, Masini committed a couple of brutal murder/rapes on two of his elderly relatives.

The first to die was his 85-year-old aunt, Anna Masini. According to Masini's later confession, he arrived at the old woman's house under the pretense of using her telephone. After drinking a soda, he was washing out his glass in the kitchen sink, when he saw a knife nearby. He picked up the weapon and without warning, began stabbing his aunt, delivering numerous wounds to her neck. He then raped her corpse, both vaginally and anally. He said later that he felt "detached" during the entire episode.

Two weeks later, Masini called at the home of another elderly relative, Angelina Ialeggio. Following the 80-year-old to the kitchen, he picked up a knife and stabbed her to death, before raping her and robbing her of a ring.

A year passed before Masini struck again, this time killing an elderly couple, Michael Krieger, 83, and his 78-year-old wife, Betty, who had employed him to do some carpentry work. On the day before Thanksgiving, 1992, Masini arrived at the Kriegers' home, ostensibly to do some work. At some point during the day, he attacked the couple, stabbing them to death and raping Mrs. Krieger posthumously.

The Kriegers were due at a Thanksgiving party the following evening and when they didn't show, their son drove to their West Orange home and found their bodies.

It was immediately clear to the officers responding to the call that the Kriegers must have known their assailant. The couple was described by their son as "extremely security conscious," and yet there was no sign of forced entry to the home. Then, after investigators learned from a neighbor that Masini's truck had been parked outside all day, he was hauled in for questioning. He soon confessed to the murders.

In April 1990, Frank Masini pled guilty to the murders of Anna Masini, Angelina Ialeggio, and Michael and Betty Krieger. He was sentenced to four life terms, with parole eligibility after 30 years. No satisfactory explanation has ever been given for his killing spree.

Edward McGregor

On the evening of April 17, 1990, the 911 dispatcher in Missouri City, Texas, received a chilling call. The clearly distressed woman on the other end of the line said that she had been stabbed and that she was dying. "Do you know the man who attacked you?" the dispatcher asked. "No, I'm dying, please come," the caller gasped.

Tracing the address to the 1400 block of Whispering Pines, the dispatcher immediately sent a unit. They arrived to find 38-year-old Kim Wildman lying on the floor. She'd been savagely raped and then stabbed to death. Evidence at the scene suggested that she'd put up a fierce struggle for her life. In the end, though, her attacker had just been too strong.

Four years later, on May 25, 1994, Edwina Barnum, 23, came home from working a late shift at her job. She arrived at her Houston apartment, unlocked the door and stepped inside. Probably, she slipped off her shoes, slumped into a chair and relaxed a while. Maybe she considered getting a snack before heading to bed. Except there would be no snack, no quiet time, no peaceful night's sleep.

At around, 2:20 a.m., a neighbor noticed Barnum's door standing ajar. It appeared to have been forced. He summoned the building manager, who found the young woman dead in her bedroom. She'd been strangled and shot in the head. She'd also been raped, and crime scene technicians were able to lift semen from the scene, which delivered a DNA profile. No match was found on record.

On August 5, 2005, over a decade since the Barnum murder, Danielle Subjects rose as normal, got her two young kids washed, dressed, and fed, and then delivered them to daycare. She then returned to her apartment to get ready for work.

At approximately 1 p.m., her roommate returned to the apartment and found the door standing ajar. Thinking that Danielle must still be at home, she entered, but her calls brought no reply. She soon found out why. Danielle's brutalized body lay in the bath, beaten, strangled, and deliberately posed.

Mandy Rubin, like Danielle Subjects, was the single mother of two young children. Like Subjects, she also lived in an apartment in southwest Houston and, like Subjects, she also fell prey to a vicious predator. Mandy was found in her bathtub on February 4, 2006. She'd been raped and strangled, her body posed for shock value. No sign of forced entry to the apartment was found, indicating perhaps that she had known her attacker.

As in the previous murders, the police retrieved semen from the crime scene, but again this produced no match. Then they hit on another idea. If Mandy Rubin had known her attacker and had willingly admitted him to the apartment, what were the chances that he lived close by? Perhaps even in the same building?

With this in mind, they asked the male residents of the apartment block to voluntarily submit a blood sample for DNA analysis. The residents were, of course, at liberty to refuse but if anyone did, that might in itself provide a clue, a focal point for the investigation.

As it turned out, no one refused and the police soon had a match, a 29-year-old man who lived in the building – Edward McGregor. DNA also linked McGregor to the 2005 murder of Danielle Subjects, the killing of Edwina Bartram, and the murder of Kim Wildman in 1990, when McGregor would have been just 17-years-old.

Tried and found guilty, McGregor was sentenced to life in prison. Yet investigators are curious about the long gaps between the murders, and as McGregor has spent time in Florida, Georgia, and Louisiana, they are looking into unsolved homicides there.

Johnny Meadows

Between October 1968 and June 1971, the town of Odessa Texas was plagued by a sadistic sex slayer, a fiend who raped, stabbed, and strangled his victims, then disappeared into the night with nary a clue left behind.

The deadly spree began on October 19, 1968. On that evening Odessa barmaid Linda Cougat took a load of washing to a local Laundromat and promptly vanished without trace. Her badly decomposed corpse was found two months later, in a field northwest of town. Her hands were bound behind her back with one of her own nylon stockings. The other was wrapped tightly around her throat.

Just over two weeks later, on November 5, 1968, police were summoned to an apartment in nearby Monahans, Texas, where motel owner Dorothy Smith had been found strangled to death. Smith was lying on the floor, her hands bound with a television cord, another length of cable forming a ligature around her neck.

The next to die was Eula Miller, found nude in her Odessa apartment on July 16, 1970, with multiple stab wounds to her neck and torso. And then there was Nancy Miller, abducted from her home in Kermit on September 16, while her children slept in the next room. Her skeletal remains turned up almost a year later, on the site of an oil lease to the south of town.

Before that discovery, another woman was murdered. Ruth Maynard was the wife of an Odessa police officer. She went missing from her home on January 17, 1971. Her brutalized corpse was found on February 15, just a few miles from where Linda Cougat had been discovered.

With the small town now virtually in a state of siege, another woman disappeared on June 17. Gloria Green worked as a secretary in the neighboring town of Kermit, Texas. Her disappearance brought the number of dead and missing women to six. And still, the police had no leads, nor any idea who the elusive serial killer might be.

Then, just when they were beginning to believe that the killer would never be caught, the case unexpectedly resolved itself.

In January 1972, a man named Johnny Meadows was arrested in Fort Worth, Texas. Shortly after his incarceration, Meadows asked to speak with the sheriff of Ector County, claiming he had information that would clear up a homicide committed there the previous year. The tip-off was conveyed to Sheriff A.M. Gambrel, who immediately flew to Fort Worth to question Meadows.

100

Meadows was initially cagey, but then began providing details about the murder of an unnamed woman, who the sheriff soon realized was Gloria Green.

According to Meadows he knew the location of the body, and would divulge it on payment of $2,000 to his wife. The money duly changed hands and, following Meadows' directions, officers went to a vacant lot in South Odessa, where Green's skeletal remains lay beneath a rotting mattress.

Meadows was charged with murder, and against his attorney's advice, signed a full confession to the crime, as well as the murders of Linda Cougat, Dorothy Smith, and Ruth Maynard.

Tried only for the murder of Gloria Green, he was found guilty and sentenced to 99 years in prison.

Benjamin Franklin Miller Jr.

Serial killers, as a general rule, prey on victims of their own race and sexual orientation. White heterosexual men tend to target white heterosexual women; black heterosexual men tend to prey on black women of similar orientation; gay serial killers tend to target other homosexuals.

There are, of course, exceptions to the rule but where they exist they are most often black killers who target white victims (Carlton Gary, Coral Watts, and Cleophus Prince spring to mind, but there are many others). Benjamin Miller Jr. is, therefore, a rarity, a white serial killer who exclusively targeted African American women.

Between the years 1967 and 1971, the African American citizens of Stamford, Connecticut, were terrorized by a brutal strangler who throttled five young women to death with their own brassieres. The fact that all of the victims were prostitutes, and some of them known drug addicts, did nothing to calm community fears. Every black woman in Stamford felt like she was a potential victim. Worse still, it appeared that the police were not investigating the case with the vigor it deserved.

The "Bra Strangler" had first announced his deadly presence on August 4, 1967, when the body of 29-year-old Rosell "Sissy" Rush was found strangled in a wooded area, off the Merritt Parkway in Stamford.

Donna Roberts, aged 22, was the next to die, her strangled corpse discovered on May 3, 1968, the day after her disappearance.

Four months later another young woman, 21-year-old Gloria Khan, was found strangled to death at a site just 200 feet from the spot where Roberts had been found. The killer then went to ground, raising hopes that he'd died or been caught for another crime. Not so. He re-emerged three years later to strangle 19-year-old Gail Thompson, on July 10, 1971.

He struck again 6 weeks later, on August 22, throttling 34-year-old Alma Henry, and discarding her body within the same quarter-mile radius where all of the victims had been found.

By now, anger within the black community had reached boiling point and the police responded by assembling a task force of state and local officers to work the case. During the course of their investigation, task force detectives were alerted to Benjamin Miller, a white postal worker from Darien. Convinced that they were hunting a black man, investigators were at first skeptical of this tip.

However, as they started looking into Miller's background, some interesting information began to emerge. They learned, for example, that Miller had a history of psychiatric problems and spent much of his time preaching on the streets. They learned also that he had been involved in relationships with a number of black women.

Miller was pulled in for questioning and interrogated at length. He denied involvement in the murders, admitting only that he'd had sexual relations with Gail Thompson in his car.

Despite Miller's denials, many of his responses aroused suspicion, as he mentioned details about the murders that had not been released to the public. Asked to submit to a polygraph, Miller readily agreed. The results were inconclusive.

On February 16, Miller was checked into Fairfield Hills psychiatric hospital after it was found that he was suffering from chronic undifferentiated schizophrenia. While he was at Fairfield he was interviewed several times by Dr. Robert Miller (no relation).

On February 29, Dr. Miller contacted task force detectives and advised them that the suspect wished to talk to them. In the ensuing interview, Miller confessed to seven murders.

Benjamin Miller was subsequently found not guilty by reason of insanity. He was committed to a State mental institution to be retained indefinitely.

Blanche Taylor Moore

Blanche Taylor Moore (nee Kiser) was born in Tarheel, North Carolina, on February 17, 1933. Her father, Parker D. Kiser, was a mill-worker and self-proclaimed preacher with an appetite for booze, women, and gambling. By the time Blanche reached her teens, he was farming her out as a prostitute to pay off his gambling debts.

Marrying young to escape her father's abuse, Blanche tied the knot with James Taylor in May 1952, and over the years bore him two daughters, Vanessa in 1953 and Cindi in 1959. Blanche had in the interim found work as a checker at the Kroger supermarket in Burlington, and by 1959 had been promoted to head cashier.

All was not well on the home front, however. James Taylor had turned out to be a younger version of Blanche's father, a hard-drinking gambler who made a habit of blowing his family's housekeeping money on poker and horse racing. In retaliation, Blanche conducted a series of affairs with her male colleagues at the supermarket.

In 1962, she turned her romantic attentions on Raymond Reid, the newly appointed assistant manager at Kroger. Reid was married and had two young children but Blanche was not put off, pursuing her man for three years before eventually bedding him.

In September 1966, Blanche reconciled with her father, just in time as it turned out, because he died soon after. His death was put down to a heart attack, but his symptoms - severe stomach cramps, diarrhea, projectile vomiting, and delirium, were inconsistent with that diagnosis.

Blanche's husband, meanwhile, had undergone a conversion to Christianity and given up booze and gambling, leading Blanche to describe him to all who would listen as, 'the perfect husband.' Taylor's transformation, though, did nothing to discourage her ongoing affair with Raymond Reid. Reid eventually abandoned his wife and children for Blanche in 1970. By then, another person in Blanche's immediate circle, her mother-in-law Isla Taylor, was dead. Blanche had nursed the old woman during the last months of her life.

Within a year, James Taylor, too, was dead. Having developed flu-like symptoms in September 1971, he soon developed diarrhea, swollen glands, and hair loss. Painful blisters appeared on his hands and feet and there was blood in his stool and urine. He died in hospital on October 2, shortly after Blanche brought him some ice cream from home.

Following Taylor's death, Blanche began openly dating Raymond Reid. He spoke of marriage but she kept putting him off. In truth, she'd tired of her paramour. Her sights were now set higher.

Blanche next honed in on Kroger store manager Kevin Denton. When that flirtation soured, she filed a sexual harassment suit against Denton and Kroger, forcing Denton to resign and her employer to pay up $275,000 in an out-of-court settlement. Next, Blanche turned her never-ending quest for cash to insurance fraud, netting two payouts due to fires at her home.

In April 1985, there was a new man in her life, Rev. Dwight Moore, pastor of the Carolina United Church of Christ. There was an obstacle to the relationship, though. Raymond Reid was still in the picture, still hoping that Blanche would accept his marriage proposal.

In early 1986, Reid developed shingles. By April, he was hospitalized with diarrhea, vomiting, and loss of feeling in his hands and feet. By October he was dead, his body having gained sixty pounds in retained body fluids, bloating so severely that it caused his skin to rip.

Blanche had been a constant visitor during his hospitalization, bringing him regular food treats from home. She netted $30,000 from Reid's estate, plus $45,797 from life insurance.

With Reid out of the picture, Blanche stepped up her pursuit of the Reverend Moore. Their wedding was set for August 23, 1987, but was postponed after Blanche was diagnosed with breast cancer and had to undergo a mastectomy.

The wedding was rearranged for November 27, 1988. About three weeks before that date, Moore was suddenly stricken with vomiting and diarrhea, resulting in another postponement. Eventually, on April

21, 1989, the nuptials were completed and the newlyweds honeymooned in Montclair, New Jersey.

Back home on April 26, Dwight collapsed after eating a pastry. He was admitted to North Carolina Memorial, where a toxicology screen turned up copious amounts of arsenic, over 20 times the lethal dosage.

Despite Moore's protestations that his wife would never harm him, Blanche was questioned by police on June 6. As a result of that interview, exhumations were ordered on Raymond Reid, James Taylor, Parker D. Kiser, and Isla Taylor. All showed evidence of arsenic poisoning.

Blanche Taylor Moore was tried for the murder of Raymond Reid in 1990. Despite her pleas of innocence, she was found guilty and sentenced to death. She remains on death row over two decades later.

Hugh Morse

Hugh Morse had the worst possible start in life. Born in Kansas City, Missouri, in January 1930, Morse was the product of a shotgun marriage. His father abandoned the family shortly after his birth, leaving the boy to the tender mercies of a staggeringly brutal grandmother. When he was four, grandma delivered a blow to his head with a hammer, leaving him carrying a facial scar that would be with him for life. On another occasion, she killed his beloved pet mice after he sneaked out to a movie without her permission.

Given this background, it is unsurprising that Morse grew up with deeply ambivalent feelings towards women. On the one hand, their ability to hurt and dominate, terrified him. One the other, he carried a deep-seated hatred for the abuse meted out to him. It provided a fertile breeding ground for the creation of a sexual psychopath.

As soon as he was old enough, Morse left home to enlist in the Marine Corps. However, his military career would be a short one. Arrested in May 1951, for an assault on a woman in Wilmington, North Carolina, he was dishonorably discharged, having served less than a year.

More arrests followed in civilian life, although none of them stuck until Morse was picked up on a burglary charge in Los Angeles, and sentenced to six months.

Shortly after his release in 1955, Morse was in trouble again, this time for the attempted rape of two eight-year-old girls in Fairfield, California. Committed to Atascadero State Hospital, he was pronounced "cured" eighteen months later, and released. He'd enjoy just four months of freedom before being picked up again for sexual assault.

Morse had by now developed a distinct M.O. His favorite approach was to break into homes at night and surprise sleepy female residents in their beds. However, the L.A.P.D. were by now onto him, so he absconded to Spokane, Washington. There, he married, although the union was short-lived.

With his wife out of the picture, Taylor began prowling again. On November 7, 1959, he invaded the Spokane home of 28-year-old Glorie Brie, raped her and then strangled her to death. He struck again on September 26, 1960, killing 69-year-old Blanche Boggs. Two weeks later, he raped Beverly Myers and attempted to stab her to death. She survived, albeit with deep physical and mental scars.

On October 28, 1960, Morse broke into the home of his estranged wife and tried to strangle her. Interrupted during the course of the attack, he was forced to flee, whereupon his wife promptly called the police and reported the crime.

With a federal warrant out for his arrest, Morse hit the road. On August 29, 1961, he was placed on the FBI's "Ten Most Wanted" list.

In the spring of 1961, Morse was arrested for peeping into windows in Atlanta, Georgia. He paid the $200 bail and walked away free, the officers apparently unaware that it was his face staring down at them from the wanted poster on the precinct wall.

On July 11, 1961, Morse broke into a home in Birmingham, Alabama, and choked Bobbi Ann Landini into unconsciousness before battering her to death with a length of pipe. Three weeks later, he attacked Mildred Chasteen in her Dayton apartment. Somehow, she survived the multiple stab wounds inflicted on her.

Morse next showed up in St. Paul, Minnesota, under the alias "Darwin Corman." On September 18, he raped and strangled Carol Ronan in her home, five blocks from the rooming house where he was staying. A few days later, he lured a six-year-old girl into an alley and sexually molested her.

But time was running out for Hugh Morse. On September 29, an anonymous tip-off to the local FBI office brought the Feds to his door. Morse surrendered without a fight and under questioning confessed to killing Carol Ronan. He was sentenced to life in prison for that murder, with the states of Washington and Alabama waiting to prosecute him should he ever be released.

Eric Napoletano Jr.

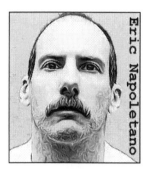

In the summer of 1964, Carolyn Hankinson, a 24-year old auxiliary officer with the NYPD, met a man named Eric Ernest Napoletano in a New York City bar. The two began a brief affair during which Carolyn became pregnant. Napoletano, though, wasn't too keen on the responsibilities of fatherhood. He was long gone by the time his son was born on May 2, 1965. Undaunted by her lover's desertion, Carolyn adopted his surname and named her baby, Eric Ernest Napoletano Jr.

Eric's childhood was tumultuous and although his mother was absolutely devoted to him, the two fought regularly. The boy also had several spells in various mental institutions. At the age of 11, after yet another hospitalization, Eric went to live with a 48-year-old man who he had befriended. This arrangement seems to have been reached with the full cooperation of Carolyn, but although she handed over full responsibility for Eric's upbringing, she maintained a strong relationship with her son. Despite Eric's early difficulties, she was determined that he would grow up to become a New York City police officer.

When Eric was 18, he joined the Marines but was unable to make the cut and flunked out soon after. His mother was furious, warning him that it would affect his chances of being accepted into the NYPD. But Eric had never been particularly interested in a police career. He had other plans.

In 1984, the 19-year-old Eric began dating 15-year-old, Marilyn Coludro. The relationship followed a familiar pattern with Eric. He was tall and reasonably good-looking and women liked him. A string of girlfriends would later testify that he'd start out charming and attentive but soon become overly possessive and abusive. His favorite pastimes were handcuffing and sexual torture. If the women threatened to leave, he'd respond by threatening to kill her.

A few months into her relationship with Napoletano, Marilyn Coludro disappeared from her home in Queens. Her body would turn up two years later, in Pennsylvania. She'd been stabbed to death.

Eric seemed strangely unmoved by her disappearance. Shortly after, he began dating Wanda Matos and not long after, they were married.

Six months into the marriage, Wanda's mother Gladys was gunned down in the Bronx. Napoletano was the prime suspect in her murder, but he escaped arrest mainly because his mother (by now a civilian employee of the NYPD) provided him with an alibi. She also coached him in how to lie to the police.

In the wake of Gladys Matos' murder, Napoletano's marriage fell apart. By 1990 he was remarried and the father of two young sons. However, the demons that haunted Eric Napoletano were only resting, not stilled. They rose up again on June 21, 1990, when Myra Acevedo Napoletano threatened to leave him and take their boys to live with her parents in Puerto Rico. Napoletano reacted in typical fashion. After beating Myra, he looped a rope around her neck and strangled her to death in front of their children. He then dumped her body in a rural area of New Castle County, Delaware, some 15 miles south of the New Jersey border. Then he placed a call to his mother.

Carolyn seemed unconcerned that her son had just committed murder. She advised him to run and Napoletano did just that, settling eventually in Albuquerque, New Mexico. He remained there in hiding until federal agents tracked him down on March 27, 1991. His first call was to his mother who again advised him on how to handle the police.

Napoletano was extradited to New York to face trial for first-degree murder. Carolyn Napoletano faced charges of conspiracy and perverting the cause of justice when it transpired that she'd been in constant contact with her son and had been feeding him information from confidential police files. It was to save his mother from prosecution that Eric eventually struck a deal.

In June 1993, he pled guilty to the murder of Myra Acevedo Napoletano and was sentenced to life in prison. His subsequent conviction for killing Marilyn Coludro added another life term. He has never been charged with the murder of Gladys Matos but remains the only suspect in that case.

Carolyn remains his staunchest ally. "He doesn't have a mean bone in his body," she insists.

Robert Nixon

On June 29, 1936, someone broke into a room at the Devonshire Hotel in Chicago, Illinois, and bludgeoned the occupant, 24-year-old Florence Castle, to death with a brick. The killer then picked up a tube of lipstick and scrawled the words "Black Legion Game," on a mirror, before exiting the way he'd come, and escaping down a fire escape. The entire attack was witnessed by the victim's 7-year-old son, who later described the killer to investigators as a "white man painted black."

As police processed the crime scene they were able to lift a clear set of fingerprints. However, the prints couldn't be matched to anything they had on file. In any case, the killer, an 18-year-old black youth named Robert Nixon, had already skipped town, bound for California.

Arriving in Los Angeles, Nixon adopted the alias Thomas Crosby and soon became known to L.A.P.D. detectives as a petty thief and second-story man. During 1937, he was arrested four times for various minor offenses. Soon he'd return to murder.

On March 2, 1937, 20-year-old Rose Valdez was attacked and beaten to death in her home by a brick-wielding assailant. A few days later, Zoe Damrell met a similar fate, the bloodied murder weapon found just outside her bedroom window. And on April 4, police were called to yet another gruesome murder scene. Edna Warden and her 12-year-old daughter, Marguerite, lay battered to death in their apartment, their blood and brain matter spattered on the floor, walls and furnishings. As in the earlier cases, the victims had been killed by repeated blows with a brick.

With the Los Angeles newspapers trumpeting lurid headlines about the murderous "Brick Moron," and the police and citizenry on high alert, Nixon slipped out of the city and headed back to his native Chicago. There, on May 27, 1938, he committed one final outrage, bludgeoning Florence Johnson to death with his favored weapon.

Shortly after the Johnson murder, Nixon was picked up on an unrelated charge and his fingerprints were matched to those found at the Castle murder scene.

Nixon initially denied responsibility for the murder, laying the blame on a 19-year-old accomplice named Earl Hicks. But under intense and sustained interrogation, he eventually cracked and confessed to killing Castle and Florence Johnson. He even accompanied detectives to the crime scenes and demonstrated how he'd scrambled up the fire escapes to gain access to the apartments.

Nixon still hadn't confessed to the Los Angeles murders, but when L.A.P.D. detectives got to hear of his arrest, they suspected that he might be the man responsible for the murders in their city. A fingerprint comparison soon proved that this was the case. California authorities immediately requested that Nixon be extradited to stand trial there, a request that was turned down by their Illinois counterparts.

Nixon was charged only with the murder of fireman's wife, Florence Johnson. He was found guilty and sentenced to die in the electric chair. After several stays of execution, that sentence was eventually carried out on June 15, 1939.

George Howard Putt

George Howard "Buster" Putt was born in New Orleans, Louisiana, in February 1946. Both of his parents were petty criminals and scam artists and the family was always on the move. George and his siblings seldom, if ever, attended school.

After Putt's parents were busted for passing bad checks, the seven children were deposited with their grandparents in North Carolina. That arrangement lasted only a short while before the grandparents deposited the entire litter of Putt children at an orphanage in Richmond, Virginia. After a number of escape attempts, George eventually landed at the Richmond Home for Boys, where it was noted that he had "a morbid preoccupation with blood and gore." He was also described as "seriously disturbed."

By the time Putt was 16, he had been arrested on two charges of attempted rape and sent to a maximum-security juvenile facility in Texas. A psychiatrist there described him as "a psychopath capable of committing almost any crime," but that didn't stop the authorities releasing him at age 21.

Upon his release, Putt drifted to Mississippi and later to Memphis, Tennessee, where he married his brother's pregnant ex-girlfriend, Mary Bulimore. Together with baby George Jr., the couple moved next to Tupelo, Mississippi, where, in May 1969, Putt was arrested for burglary.

Sentenced to six months he soon escaped and fled with his family to Memphis, Tennessee. There the couple struggled to make ends meet, with Putt working various menial jobs. He supplemented his meager earnings with petty thefts and after losing yet another job due to stealing, George Putt finally seemed to crack. Over the next two months, he launched a bloody campaign of murder that remains one of the most brutal the city has seen.

On August 14, 1969, 23-year-old Putt gained access to the home of disabled World War II veteran Roy Dumas and his wife Bernalyn. Inside he bound and gagged the couple before killing them in a murder so brutal that the police refused to release details. It later emerged that Mrs. Dumas had been sexually mutilated with a pair of scissors. The motive, though, appeared to be robbery, as the house had been ransacked. A partial fingerprint was left at the scene.

Twelve days passed before Putt struck again, killing 80-year-old Leila Jackson. Mrs. Jackson was strangled and sexually mutilated, a lamp positioned to shine on her body so that it highlighted the killer's macabre handiwork.

With the city now gripped by fear, Putt waited five days before abducting 21-year-old Glenda Sue Harden on her way to work. A massive manhunt was launched and eventually turned up Harden's body in Riverside Park. She'd been stabbed 14 times in the back, chest, neck, and head.

One hundred and thirty-five detectives were now working the case. Meanwhile, city authorities posted a $20,000 reward and appealed to the FBI for help. It did no good.

On September 11, 1969, Putt was skulking around an apartment building at 41 North Bellevue. He'd already tried, and failed, to talk himself into Grace Oldham's apartment when he spotted Christine Pickens, celebrating her 59th birthday that day. Forcing Pickens into her home, he began attacking her. Pickens managed to call out and one of her neighbors went to her aid. As the woman arrived, she saw Putt step from the apartment into the hallway carrying a bloody knife. Putt fled the scene, with three other neighbors in hot pursuit, one of them firing at Putt as he ran.

The shots drew police officers Glenn Noblin and Phil Scruggs and they caught the killer on Linden Avenue, his hands and clothes spattered in blood. Christine Pickens had meanwhile died from the 20 stab wounds inflicted on her.

Despite being caught (quite literally) red-handed, Putt continued to maintain his innocence for 48 hours before he eventually confessed. He later recanted but was tried and found guilty anyway. He was sentenced to death, the sentence later commuted to life in prison after the Supreme Court outlawed capital punishment in 1972.

Putt is currently serving his sentence at the Turney Center Industrial Prison in Only, Tennessee. He is required to serve a minimum of 437 years before becoming eligible for parole.

Andre Rand

Born Frank Rashan in Manhattan on March 11, 1944, Andre Rand was a pedophilic serial killer who went by the ominous moniker, "The Pied Piper of Staten Island." He grew up in Ithaca, New York, served in the Army during the early 1960s, and was employed as a physical therapy aide at New York's Willowbrook State School from 1966 to 1968. Thereafter, he worked at odd jobs, while living in various rooming houses on Staten Island.

His first brush with the law came on May 25, 1969, when he lured a 9-year-old into his vehicle and drove her to a vacant lot. A passing police cruiser found him and the little girl naked in the car and he was charged with attempted rape and sentenced to 16 months in prison. Released in 1972, he legally changed his name to "Andre Rand."

In 1972, Rand was working as a painter at a Staten Island apartment building when five-year-old Alice Pereira went missing. Rand was strongly suspected in the disappearance but denied any involvement and with no solid evidence linking him to the crime, the police were forced to let it drop.

He similarly escaped convictions on two rape arrests in 1979, after the victims, a young woman and a 15-year-old girl, declined to press charges.

In July 1981, Rand was pulled in for questioning regarding the disappearance of seven-year-old Holly Hughes, from Port Richmond. His green Volkswagen had been seen circling the block near the convenience store where the little girl was last seen. Rand denied being near the store and was eventually released for lack of evidence.

Also in 1981, Rand attempted to lure a 9-year-old into his car by offering her a lollipop. When the girl refused, he continued stalking her until she ran home and hid under a rug. Rand was questioned about the incident but not charged.

On January 9, 1983, Rand drove a group of eleven Staten Island children to Newark Airport, to watch the planes landing and taking off. None of the children were harmed, but Rand had not obtained parental permission and found himself charged with unlawful imprisonment. He served 10 months in jail.

Rand was back on the streets by August and listed as a suspect when 10-year-old Tiahese Jackson vanished from a Staten Island street. Tiahese had still not been found when 12-year-old Down's Syndrome sufferer, Jennifer Schweiger, disappeared from her home in Westerleigh on July 9, 1987.

This time, though, Rand had slipped up. Several witnesses came forward to say that they had seen him leading the trusting little girl by the hand toward the woods at Willowbrook, where he was living in a makeshift shelter. In short order, Rand found himself under arrest, charged with kidnapping.

In the meanwhile, the police conducted a massive search of the Willowbrook grounds and eight days later discovered Jennifer's body in a shallow grave. She'd been buried within sight of Rand's lean-to.

Rand went on trial in 1989, was found guilty of first-degree murder, and sentenced to 25 years to life. The bodies of Alice Pereira, Holly Hughes, and Tiahese Jackson have never been recovered and Rand continues to deny publically that he was involved in their disappearances. To his prison buddies, though, he's been known to boast about the murders, and to liken himself to Ted Bundy.

Alonzo Robinson

Alonzo Robinson had two obsessions in life. One was writing obscene letters, considered a serious offense in the 1920's and 30's, but paling into insignificance when compared to his other favorite pastime. That involved serial murder, with a penchant for necrophilia and cannibalism thrown in. He also enjoyed holding onto keepsakes from his victims – usually their severed heads.

It is difficult to ascertain what turned Robinson into the monster he would become. Very little is known about his upbringing except that he was born on the wrong side of the tracks in Cleveland, Mississippi. He first came to police attention in 1918, when a series of obscene letters sent to local women was traced back to him. Officers arrived to arrest Robinson but despite taking a bullet in the shoulder, he escaped.

Eight years later, police in Ferndale, Michigan, were stumped by a baffling series of crimes. Headless female corpses had begun turning up all over town, four by the time the investigation honed in on a man named James Coyner. Coyner was in fact, Alonzo Robinson, but by the time investigators arrived to question him, he'd flown the coop. He left behind adequate proof of his guilt, though. Four severed heads were found inside his house.

Michigan detectives eventually tracked Robinson to Indiana where he was serving a prison term for grave robbing. Robinson denied that he was James Coyner and claimed to have no knowledge of the Ferndale murders. With insufficient evidence to support a murder charge, the investigators were forced to let the matter drop.

Paroled in July 1934, Robinson again assumed the identity "James Coyner," and returned to his hometown of Cleveland, Mississippi. There he picked up his old hobby of writing obscene letters.

One of those letters went to an Indianapolis woman, who reported it to the authorities. Federal investigators were called in and soon picked up a clue. There was an error in the woman's address that was identical to a recent misprint in a local newspaper. Agents began scanning the paper's subscription list in the hope of catching the pornographer.

Robinson, meanwhile, had turned his attentions back to murder. On December 8, 1934, Aurelius Turner and his wife were shot dead in their Cleveland home. Mrs. Turner's body was severely mutilated, with chunks of flesh hacked from the corpse and carried from the scene.

In January 1935, federal agents eventually linked the Indianapolis letter to James Coyner, his address given as a post box in Shaw, Mississippi. They were waiting to arrest "Coyner" when he arrived to pick up his mail on January 12, 1935. A search of his pockets turned up a .38 revolver and a number of obscene letters.

But it was only after agents searched Robinson's house that they finally understood the nature of the man they'd been pursuing. Among the macabre artifacts discovered there, were swatches of human hair and strips of human flesh, salted and cured like beef jerky.

Robinson freely confessed to the murders of Mr. and Mrs. Turner. He also admitted to keeping the heads found in his home in Michigan although he insisted they were from corpses he'd dug up, rather than from murder victims.

History does not record the fate of Alonzo Robinson, which likely means that he was declared unfit to stand trial and was committed to a mental institution.

Helmuth Schmidt

A "Bluebeard" is a unique type of serial killer, a man who preys on gullible women, enticing them with promises of love and security, fleecing them of their belongings and then dispatching them, before moving on to the next victim. The term derives from the fairy tale about a wealthy gentleman who lures several young maidens to his castle where he imprisons and subsequently murders them. Although the idea seems quaint today, there was a time when such killers abounded and there were many potential victims. Two famous cases involved Henri Landau of France and George Joseph Smith of England, while famous American Bluebeards include Johann Hoch and Harry Powers.

A lesser-known American case is that of Helmuth Schmidt, a German émigré to the United States who preyed on lonely, immigrant women in Missouri, New York, New Jersey, and Michigan.

Schmidt's M.O. was simplicity itself. Using various aliases, he would take out newspaper ads in lonely heart's columns, describing himself as a wealthy man in search of a wife. The women he attracted were in the main poorly educated, German immigrants, many of them employed as domestic servants. No doubt they hoped for a better life. What they got instead was a swift and brutal death.

Schmidt would invite the girls to his residence to discuss the prospect of matrimony. Once there, he'd murder them and relieve them of their meager belongings, then he'd bury them in a pre-dug grave in the cellar and fill it in with cement. He'd then disappear before anyone could ask questions. Then he'd run the ruse all over again. The motive was primarily financial, but as Bluebeard serial killer Harry Powers attested years later, there is definitely a sexual element to such crimes as well.

In 1918, Schmidt fled New York after a friend of one of his victims, Augusta Steinbach, reported her missing to the police and named Schmidt as a possible suspect. Steinbach had answered an ad placed by Schmidt in the New York Herald and had subsequently arranged to meet him. She'd never returned from that meeting.

Schmidt made his way to Royal Oak, Michigan, and found work at the Ford plant just outside of Detroit. He also began his old ruse of placing lonely heart ads in the local newspaper.

But time was almost up for Helmuth Schmidt. On April 23, 1918, New York detectives traced him to Michigan and took him into custody. Schmidt staunchly denied any wrongdoing, even when detectives produced items of Steinbach's bloody clothing, which had been found hidden under the porch at his former residence.

He must have known the game was up, though. That night he committed suicide in his cell by pulling a heavy iron bedstead down on his head, crushing his skull.

No one will ever know how many women Helmuth Schmidt lured to their deaths, although contemporary accounts put the number at 30 plus.

Beoria Simmons III

If there is one facet of the justice system that angers capital punishment advocates it is the amount of time that condemned felons remain alive on death row before the sentence of the court is carried out.

In some states, Texas and Virginia for example, justice moves fairly quickly and an execution might be carried out in five to seven years. In others (California being a case in point) a condemned inmate is more likely to die of old age than by lethal injection.

The problem lies in the number of state and federal appeals a prisoner is allowed, often resulting in an execution being delayed for decades. Defense attorneys, of course, are well aware of this and play the system to the hilt. A classic example is the case of Beoria Simmons.

Few criminals can have been more deserving of the death penalty than
Simmons. A brutal rapist and murderer, Simmons snuffed out the lives
of three young women in a reign of terror lasting from 1981 to 1983.

The first victim was 15-year Robin Barnes. Abducted at gunpoint near
her home in Louisville, Kentucky, on May 18, 1981, Robin was driven
to Iroquois Park where she was beaten, raped and sodomized.
Simmons then ended her life with two bullets, one to the chest and
another that entered under her chin and exited at her temple. Her body
was discovered in the park three days later.

Simmons would claim two more victims before his eventual arrest on
June 11, 1983. Shannon House, 29, was abducted, raped and killed on
March 25, 1982; Nancy Bettman, 39, met a similar fate on March 11,
1983. Both of their bodies were dumped in Iroquois Park.

There is little doubt that Simmons would have continued his murder
campaign, but he bit off more than he could chew with his next victim.
The 16-year-old girl was snatched from a street in Churchill Downs
and driven to Iroquois Park. There, Simmons calmly told her that he
was going to rape her and would let her go if she co-operated.
Unfortunately for him, his intended victim was armed with a knife and
as he made his move she stabbed him and made her getaway. The
heroic teen later reported the crime and her description led police to
Simmons.

Simmons was tried and condemned to die in the electric chair on May
13, 1985, and that should have been the end of the story. However, his
legal team managed to delay his fate for a quarter of a century, with a
succession of appeals and petitions.

Eventually, in 2010, prosecutors began to fear that a new trial would see Simmons walk free. Twenty-nine years had elapsed since the murder of Robin Barnes. Many of the detectives and witnesses from the original trial were dead. Those who were still alive might have their recall of events called into question by the defense.

The difficult decision was therefore made to offer Simmons life in prison, in exchange for dropping all further appeals. Simmons quickly agreed and the deal was done on March 3, 2010.

Thus the brutal killer avoided the punishment assigned to him, offering these empty words to the families of his victims.

"I just want to say I'm sorry for all the grief and pain I've caused throughout the years. You know, if I could undo it, I'd undo it. But I can't, so I pray to God he'd bless you all, you know, just bring some peace to your life."

Robert Spangler

On the morning of December 30, 1978, Arapahoe County deputies arrived at a residence in Littleton, Colorado, to investigate a brutal triple murder. A neighbor had discovered the bodies of 45-year-old Nancy Spangler, her 17-year-old son, David, and 15-year-old daughter, Susan. All three had suffered gunshot wounds from a .38-caliber handgun. David and Susan were found in their beds, Nancy, slumped over a typewriter in the basement with a bullet wound to her temple. A typewritten suicide note lay on the table beside her.

It was all set up to look like a murder/suicide, but the investigating officers weren't buying it, especially after the husband, Robert Spangler, changed his story several times and was found to have gunshot residue on his hand. Spangler readily admitted that he'd been having marital problems, but denied any involvement in the killings, claiming he'd been at work at the time. He explained the residue away by saying he'd handled the gun after it had been fired. A polygraph was administered and proved inconclusive. With no evidence to prove otherwise, the Arapahoe County coroner was forced to declare the case a double homicide/suicide.

Within seven months, Spangler had remarried. He and his new wife enjoyed a mutual love of the outdoors and spent much time hiking the Grand Canyon. But the relationship eventually broke down and the couple divorced in 1988.

In 1990, Spangler married Donna Sundling. The third Mrs. Spangler was an active 54-year-old, an aerobics instructor, with five grown children from her previous marriage. Spangler soon introduced her to his love of hiking.

On the morning of April 28, 1993, Robert Spangler appeared at a ranger station in Grand Canyon National Park and calmly told the duty officer that his wife had fallen to her death. He said that they had stopped to take a picture on the trail. He looked away for only a moment. When he looked back, his wife had disappeared.

A rescue team was called in and located Donna's body at the bottom of a 160-foot drop. She had sustained massive injuries, including multiple fractures of the neck, chest, and legs. However, the death was ruled an accident and Spangler was never investigated.

After Donna's death, Spangler reconciled with his second wife, Sharon Cooper, who moved back into his Colorado home. Sharon died of a drug overdose in 1994. Her death was recorded as a suicide.

In January 1999, cold case investigators from various jurisdictions met with federal agents in Flagstaff, Arizona. One of the cases that came under discussion was the Spangler murder/suicide. Although officially closed, the case had never been resolved to the satisfaction of Arapahoe County investigators.

After looking over the case files and learning that Robert Spangler had recently been diagnosed with inoperable brain cancer, the Feds recommended that the investigative team should approach Spangler for an interview. They believed that Spangler might be willing to unburden himself, given his terminal condition.

Spangler agreed to meet Arapahoe County detectives and FBI agents at the local sheriff's office. The strategy employed by the investigators was somewhat risky. They decided to appeal to Spangler's vanity by telling him that they wanted to interview him because he was a unique killer.

Amazingly, it worked. After taking the night to think it over, Spangler returned the following morning and admitted to killing his wife and children. The motive, he said, was so that he could marry Sharon Cooper. He didn't want the hassle of a messy divorce.

The investigative team now had him on three counts of premeditated murder, but Spangler staunchly denied involvement in the overdose death of Sharon Cooper. He also refused to discuss the death of his third wife, Donna Sundling, because he feared an unlawful death suit by her children.

Again an unorthodox approach loosened his tongue. The investigators told Spangler that he would not be classified a serial killer based on three murders in a single incident. Spangler contemplated for a moment, then grinned and said, "You've got your serial." He then admitted to planning and carrying out his scheme to murder Donna by pushing her off the ledge.

Spangler would eventually plead guilty to killing Nancy, David, Susan, and Donna. He was sentenced to life imprisonment without parole. He died in prison of cancer on August 5, 2001.

Bobbie Sue Terrell

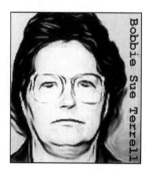

Bobbie Sue Terrell was born in Woodlawn, Illinois, on October 16, 1952. One of eight children, she grew up overweight, myopic, and painfully shy. She achieved above average grades at school and showed some talent for music. She was also a devout Christian and played the organ for Sunday services at her local church. After graduating high school in 1973, she chose to pursue a medical career and by 1976, she was a registered nurse.

That same year, she married Danny Dudley, but her marital bliss was short-lived, when it was discovered that she could not bear children. Determined to start a family, the couple adopted a son. By then, Bobbie Sue had been diagnosed with schizophrenia, and the Dudley's marriage was in trouble.

The incident that would eventually result in the dissolution of the marriage occurred when the couple's adopted son was hospitalized for a drug overdose. Danny Dudley accused his wife of giving the child tranquilizers that had been prescribed for her. She insisted that he had ingested them accidentally. When the couple divorced, Danny got custody of the boy.

In the aftermath of the divorce, Bobbie Sue's physical and mental health rapidly declined. In short order, she was hospitalized five times, eventually committing herself to a state mental hospital, where she spent over a year under psychiatric care.

On her release, she held a number of short-term nursing positions before finding work at Hillview Manor, a rest home in Greenville, Illinois. Before long her colleagues were reporting a number of strange incidents involving Terrell, including her bizarre habit of slashing her own vagina with a pair of scissors. Unsurprisingly, Hillview terminated her employment soon after.

In July 1984, Bobbie Sue moved to St. Petersburg, obtained a Florida nursing license and found work at North Horizon Health Center, working the 11 p.m. to 7 a.m. shift. She excelled at the job and was soon promoted to shift supervisor. But within just a few months, things had started to go horribly wrong.

Given her age, no one was particularly surprised when 97-year-old Aggie Marsh died on November 13, 1984. However, when 94-year-old Anna Larson passed away a few days later, eyebrows were raised. Anna died from an insulin overdose. The thing was, she was not diabetic and had not been prescribed the drug.

Another patient, 85-year-old Leathy McKnight, died from an insulin overdose on November 23. That same night, a mysterious fire broke

out in a hospital linen closet. Two days later, patients Mary
Cartwright, 79 and Stella Bradham, 85, were dead. The following day,
five elderly patients died in quick succession.

On November 26, an anonymous female caller suggested that the five
patients had been murdered. A day later police were called to the
hospital and found Bobbie Sue bleeding from a stab wound to her side.
She claimed that she'd been attacked by an intruder but her story
didn't add up. An investigation was launched. It resulted in Bobbie
Sue's dismissal from the hospital.

On January 31, 1985, Bobbie Sue was hospitalized in Pinellas County
for medical and psychiatric treatment. By this time, she was a prime
suspect in the deaths at North Horizon, and detectives had obtained
exhumation orders for nine patients.

Meanwhile, her nursing license had been suspended preventing her
from working at any medical facility in Florida. She had also
remarried, tying the knot with 38-year-old plumber Ron Terrell. The
nuptials were barely concluded when she was re-admitted to a mental
ward.

Worse was to follow for Terrell. On March 17, she was formally
charged with the murder of Anna Larson. Indictments soon followed
in the deaths of Aggie Marsh, Leathy McKnight, Stella Bradham, and
Mary Cartwright.

Terrell's trial was scheduled for October 20, 1985, but her legal team
gained several postponements before the matter eventually came to
trial in 1988. On

February 23 of that year, Bobbie Sue Terrell entered guilty pleas to reduced charges of second-degree murder. She was sentenced to 65 years in prison. She died there on August 27, 2007, of natural causes.

Richard Tingler

Like many serial killers, before and since, Richard Tingler had a difficult childhood. Born out of wedlock in December 1940, he suffered severe physical and emotional abuse from a mother who was quick to remind him that he was "born in sin." It is hardly surprising therefore that Tingler left home at the earliest opportunity, joining the air force in 1959.

Tingler was posted to Alaska, but he'd been an enlisted man for only six months when he ran into trouble with both the civilian and military authorities. After going AWOL in June 1959, he and an accomplice carried out a string of burglaries in Anchorage, a spree that earned Tingler two years in a federal prison.

Released in Chillicothe, Ohio, in February 1961, Tingler hooked up again with his air force buddy and the two picked up where they'd left off. Six months later, they were arrested in Portsmouth, Ohio, and charged with 13 counts of breaking and entering.

This time, the sentence was much harsher, 15 years in the state penitentiary, although Tingler served less than three before being paroled in August 1964. He hadn't learned his lesson, though. A new string of break-ins saw him back behind bars, where he remained until February 1968.

On September 16, 1968, a couple of early-morning joggers were horrified to stumble upon four bullet-riddled corpses laid side-by-side in Cleveland's Rockefeller Park. The victims were tavern owner Joseph Zoldman, two of his employees, and a young female prostitute. It appeared that the four had been marched to the park at gunpoint, and then systematically shot. The motive was apparently to cover up a robbery at the tavern Mr. Zoldman owned

A month later, on October 20, a lone gunman walked into a diner in Columbus, Ohio, and threatened manager Phyllis Crowe and two teenage employees – Susan Pack and Jimmy Stevens. After cleaning out the register, the man forced them into a back room, where he bound their hands. He appeared about to leave when he suddenly turned back towards his terrified victims. "What the hell," he snarled, "I ain't got nothing to lose. I'm gonna kill you all."

He then began assaulting his victims, beating Pack and Stevens, strangling Phyllis Crowe into unconsciousness, leaving her for dead. She came around about a half-hour later and found that both her young employees had been shot and killed. Ballistics tests proved that the gun was the same one used to kill the four people in Cleveland, and once Phyllis Crowe identified her assailant from a mug shot, Richard Tingler found himself elevated to the FBI's "Ten Most Wanted" list.

Tingler, meanwhile, had fled to Dill City, Oklahoma, and adopted the alias Don Williams. He found work at a farm just out of town, owned by Alvin Hoffman, and proved himself to be a reliable and hard working employee.

But still, Tingler couldn't keep out of trouble, drawing attention to himself by firing at glass insulators on high-tension poles and by shooting a neighbor's dog without provocation.

The authorities had just opened a docket to deal with those complaints when Tingler killed again. On April 27, he checked into a hotel in Gilman, Illinois, with 49-year-old Brooks Hutchenson. The following morning, a maid found Hutchenson in his room, shot four times at close range. The police were called and determined that Hutchenson had also been robbed. His wallet and his vehicle were missing.

On April 29, Tingler returned to the Hoffman farm, driving Hutchenson's late-model Ford LTD. A couple of weeks later, Washita County sheriff's were preparing to question Tingler in connection with the shooting of the dog, when they received information that he might be a wanted fugitive. Calling in a team of federal officers, they arrived at the farm on May 19 and took the multiple murderer into custody. Although armed, Tingler surrendered without a fight.

Tingler was tried on six counts, found guilty, and sentenced to die. The sentence was commuted to life in 1972, when the US Supreme Court ruled capital punishment unconstitutional.

Lydia Trueblood

Lydia Trueblood was born on October 16, 1892, in Keytesville, Missouri, her family moving to Twin Falls, Idaho, in 1906, when she was 8. In Idaho, the Truebloods struck up a friendship with a local family, the Dooleys, and in time, young Robert Dooley fell in love with Lydia. In 1912, she accepted his proposal of marriage.

Shortly after the wedding, Robert and his brother Edward entered an agreement whereby each would take out life insurance, naming the other as beneficiary.

On August 9, 1915, Edward Dooley fell suddenly ill. He died just days later, his death ascribed to typhoid.

While the Dooley clan mourned their loss, Lydia and her husband received a $2,000 payout from the insurance company. Robert also adjusted the beneficiary on his own policy, naming his wife and baby daughter. Unfortunately, the toddler died soon after, apparently as a result of drinking water from a contaminated well. Then Robert Dooley, himself, fell ill, dying on October 1, 1915, from symptoms that were remarkably similar to his brother's. Again, typhoid was named as the culprit. A check of $2,000 soon landed in the lap of his grieving widow.

Lydia Trueblood was a rather plain, homely woman. But she appears to have had no problem attracting the opposite sex. Not long after Robert Dooley's death she began dating William McHaffie, a waiter at a Twin Falls restaurant. They were married in 1917, and shortly thereafter moved to Hardin, Montana. But not before Lydia convinced her husband to take out a $5,000 life insurance policy, naming her as beneficiary.

A year later, William McHaffie was dead. Lydia was expecting another windfall but was disappointed to find that McHaffie had failed to keep up the premiums, and the policy had lapsed.

Moving on to Denver, she met and married Harlan Lewis, in May 1919. Within four months of the wedding, Lewis had succumbed to gastroenteritis and the thrice-widowed Mrs. Lewis collected $5,000 from his insurers. She moved next to Pocatello, Idaho, where she tied the knot with Edward Meyer on August 10, 1919. The following day she applied for a $10,000 insurance policy on her husband's life but was turned down. Perhaps the insurance companies were aware of her tragic history.

Edward Meyer was now a hindrance to Lydia's plans for further self-enrichment. He didn't last long. By August 25, he was ill enough to require hospitalization. By September 7, he was dead.

Meyer's death was attributed to typhoid, but a local chemist, Earl Dooley, wasn't convinced. Dooley had heard about the trail of death that had followed in Lydia's wake and decided to investigate further. His tests revealed that Meyer had died of arsenic poisoning.

By the time Dooley alerted the authorities, Lydia had already fled to California. Meanwhile, exhumation orders were obtained on the other suspected victims, all of whom showed signs of arsenic poisoning.

While the Idaho authorities were preparing a case against Lydia, she was in Los Angeles, wooing Navy Petty Officer Paul Southard. The couple married in November 1920, and Lydia immediately went to work, trying to persuade Southard to take out life insurance. He refused, saying that he was adequately covered by the navy.

Not long after, Southard was transferred to Hawaii and Lydia went with him. It was there that the authorities eventually caught up with her, on May 12, 1921. Returned to Idaho, she was tried for the murder of Edward Meyer. Found guilty, she drew a sentence of 10 years to life.

But Lydia was not prepared to spend her life behind bars. On May 4, 1931, she escaped. Fleeing to Denver, Colorado, she found work as a housekeeper to Harry Whitlock, eventually marrying her employer in March 1932.

Four months later, she was arrested in Topeka, Kansas, and returned to prison. She was eventually paroled in October 1941, and lived out her days in Salt Lake City, Utah, dying in 1958.

Clarence Walker

Clarence W. Walker, born in Tennessee on February 25, 1929, got an early start to his murderous career. He was just 14 when he was convicted of manslaughter and sentenced to prison. Released in 1940 after serving seven years, he would spend the next 25 years of his life wandering the country, surviving off the proceeds of various thefts and armed robberies. Twice he ended up in prison for short spells. Yet no one thought to question him about the vicious murders that seemed to crop up wherever he put down roots. It would allow him to remain at large for over two decades claiming a minimum of fourteen victims - three in Cleveland, Ohio, four in Michigan, and seven in Illinois.

Walker was a classic sexual psychopath, a ripper who derived pleasure from literally tearing his victims apart (with some surgical skill it was said). He was an opportunistic murderer, killing young and old with equal impunity. Typical of these were the crimes he committed while living in Benton Harbor, Michigan, under the alias, "James Darnell."

On February 6, 1965, 37-year-old Mary Jones went out for a night of drinking with some friends and promptly disappeared. Nine days later, Delores Young, age 19, was kidnapped off a Benton Harbor street. Her nude, brutalized body was found in the ruins of an abandoned building on February 16.

Two weeks after that discovery, 60-year-old Amelia Boyer disappeared from the laundry where she worked. Then, on March 30, a seven-year-old girl named Diane Carter vanished from her neighborhood, the same neighborhood where "James Darnell" had taken up residence.

On April 4, the severely mutilated remains of Mary Jones, Amelia Boyer, and Diane Carter, were found clustered together in an isolated pine grove near Bainbridge Township. Jones' had been decapitated, and there were items left at the scene, which provided a link to a similar series of mutilation murders in Cleveland, Ohio.

Meanwhile, the man known as James Darnell had skipped town and headed for Chicago. A bungled robbery there a week later would result in his arrest and eventual conviction on charges of rape, armed robbery, and assault with intent to murder. The sentence of the court was 320 years, meaning that James Darnell, a.k.a. Clarence Walker, would more than likely spend the rest of his life in prison.

Authorities in Benton Harbor, meanwhile, were stymied by the series of murders committed there. In line with the pervasive thinking of the time, they believed that that the killer they sought was a white man, more than likely a doctor, given his obvious skill in dissecting his victims. Clarence Walker, black and with hardly any education at all, let alone a medical degree, never entered the picture as a suspect.

It was not until 1970, that Walker's name began to be mentioned in connection with a rash of unsolved mutilation murders across the Midwest. Investigators had evidence that implicated him in several murders, but not enough to make a conviction stick.

Walker wasn't about to help them. He refused to meet with homicide investigators, and no amount of cajoling could make him change his mind. Eventually, they were forced to let the matter drop. However, the authorities were so convinced of Walker's guilt that Ohio, Michigan, and Illinois, closed the book on 14 unsolved homicides.

James Watson

One of the most prolific "Bluebeard" killers in American history,
James Watson was born in Paris, Arkansas, in 1870. He was christened
Charles Gillam, although by the time of his birth, his natural father had
already deserted the family. As a child, Charles was told that his father
was dead. It was only at age nine, when his mother remarried, that he
learned the truth.

Watson's new stepfather was named Joseph Olden, a brutal man who
meted out cruel physical punishments to his children. This prompted
the boy to run away from home at age 12, although he was soon
tracked down and returned to his family.

Exactly when Watson began killing, and how many he killed, is
unknown. Some contemporary accounts put his victim count as high as
25, while Watson himself claimed a more modest seven kills. Then
again, he had good reason to lie.

Watson (then using the name Joseph Olden), first fell foul of the law in
1912, while living in St. Louis, Missouri. By now married to his
second wife, he was arrested for fraud, relating to some creative
accounting in his advertising business. Rather than face a trial and
possible imprisonment, he fled to Canada and adopted the name,
James Watson.

On June 12, 1913, he bigamously married Katherine Kruse in British Columbia, later deserting her. He was married again in 1918, this time to a Mrs. Watts of Winnipeg. Both Kruse and Watts were lucky, walking away with no more than a broken heart. The next Mrs. Watson would suffer more severe injuries.

In March 1918, Watson married Marie Austin in Calgary and moved with his new bride back to the United States. Marie was to become the first of his known victims, bludgeoned to death with a rock and consigned to the depths of a lake near Coeur D'Alene, Idaho.

Later that same year, Watson married a widow in Seattle, Washington, killing her just days later by pushing her over a waterfall near Spokane. He moved next to Tacoma where, in January 1919, he married and then promptly deserted Maude Goldsmith. A month later, he tied the knot with Beatrice Andrewartha.

Beatrice survived until the spring, when she drowned while visiting Lake Washington, near Seattle. Watson would later claim that something came over him, compelling him to force Beatrice's head under the water.

Two marriages later, he wed Elizabeth Prior on March 25, 1919, at Coeur D'Alene. While honeymooning near Olympia, Washington, the couple got into an argument, during which Watson knocked his wife unconscious (accidentally, he claims). Deciding then and there to finish the job, he picked up a hammer and bludgeoned Elizabeth to death.

The next to die was Bertha Goodrich, who Watson married in June 1919 (having married and deserted three other women in the interim). Like Elizabeth Prior, Bertha did not survive the honeymoon. She was bludgeoned to death and dumped in a lake near Seattle.

A month later, new bride Alice Ludvigson fell overboard and "accidently" drowned while boating with Watson near Port Townsend, Washington. The next two Mrs. Watsons survived their husband's murderous attentions before wife number 18, Nina Delaney, was found dead near El Centro, California, in January 1920. She'd been strangled and bludgeoned, her breasts and genitals slashed with a knife.

With the body count mounting, you'd have thought that the police would have been onto Watson by now. But Watson was too clever for that. He remained constantly on the move, and chose his victims carefully, preying on women without close family bonds. Ironically, it was not suspicion of murder that proved his undoing, but suspicion of infidelity.

In the spring of 1920, Watson's new wife, concerned by his nocturnal meanderings, hired a private investigator. In the course of his inquiries, the detective found a stack of marriage licenses among Watson's possessions. Believing that he'd uncovered a serial bigamist, he reported the matter to the police.

Watson was arrested on suspicion of bigamy in April and was still in custody when word came of a woman's body unearthed near Plum Station, Washington. Fearing that it might be one of his murdered wives (it wasn't), Watson called the prison authorities and asked to make a deal, a full confession in exchange for avoiding the death penalty.

He was eventually sentenced to life in prison and died at San Quentin on October 15, 1939.

Emanuel Lovell Webb

In the eyes of the popular media, a serial killer is some kind of criminal mastermind, planning his crimes in detail, stalking his victims from the shadows, carefully covering his tracks to avoid detection. It's a tantalizing image, but one that falls far short of the truth.

In the main, serial killers are of average intelligence or below, and they usually kill victims of opportunity, people who just happen to be in the wrong place at the wrong time. The reason that these killers are so difficult to catch is because they generally target strangers, and have enough "criminal smarts" to avoid detection.

Take the apparently "unsolvable" series of homicides in 1990's Bridgeport, Connecticut, for example. Over a period of four years from late 1989 until September 1993, up to fifteen Bridgeport women fell prey to a killer rapist. The murders all occurred in the city's seedy east side and, while the victims were not all known to each other, they ran in the same circles. All were drug users who liked to party.

Most of the victims were found in their own apartments, raped, strangled, and stabbed to death. Several had been mutilated. Some were found in abandoned buildings, one in a burning car. Yet despite the best efforts of the Bridgeport Police Department, they came up empty. Eventually, the killer stopped of his own accord, the trail went cold, and the investigation was mothballed.

Fast forward to the other end of the decade and cold case investigators Heitor Teixeira and Robert Sherback decided to have a crack at the case. They immediately picked up a pattern in at least 10 of the murders. In four of them, they also had trace evidence, semen lifted from victims, Sharon Cunningham, Minnie Sutton, Elizabeth Gandy, and Sheila Etheridge.

Cunningham's body had been found on April 1, 1990, in a burning car at Crescent and Bunnell streets. Sutton was found on the floor of her Webster Avenue home on March 28, 1992. Gandy's partially clothed corpse was discovered in an abandoned building on April 19, 1993. Etheridge was found two months later, at her apartment on Bishop Avenue.

The first step taken by the cold case investigators was to send the semen samples for DNA analysis. They soon had a match. All were traced to Emanuel L. Webb, a convict currently serving time for a 1994 involuntary manslaughter in Vidalia, Georgia.

As Bridgeport investigators looked into Webb's past, they instinctively knew that he was their man. The Georgia-native had lived in Bridgeport during the time of the murders. He had moved in the same circles as the victims, and may have known several of them. The killings had stopped once he returned to his home state.

The homicide he'd committed in Georgia also bore startling similarities to the Connecticut series. Evelyn Charity had been strangled and stabbed during what Webb had described as "wild sex." He'd pled to a reduced charge and served just six years. Now, though, he was being extradited to Connecticut where he faced the very real prospect of the death penalty.

Fearful of this, Webb struck a deal, pleading "no contest" to murder charges relating to the deaths of Sharon Cunningham, Minnie Sutton, and Elizabeth Gandy. Charges were dropped in the case of Sheila Etheridge.

Webb was sentenced to 60 years in prison on June 23, 2008.

Robert Weeks

Robert Weeks had a problem with rejection, a characteristic common to many serial killers, who find that their narcissistic exterior doesn't sit well with the low self-esteem that afflicts them. A native of Georgia, Weeks was an intelligent and driven man who worked his way through Mississippi Southern College while taking on part-time jobs as diverse as mortician and parachute stuntman.

In 1954, Weeks found himself in Minneapolis, Minnesota, where he met and wooed his first wife, Patricia. In 1955, attracted by the opportunities he saw in the burgeoning city of Las Vegas, he moved to Nevada. Weeks prospered there, opening the city's first limousine service in 1960.

But his gregarious, glad-handing exterior concealed another side that only his wife was privy to. Weeks suffered from pathological jealousy when it came to Patricia. The young woman was made a virtual prisoner in the couple's home, only allowed to leave if accompanied by her husband.

When Patricia complained of boredom, Weeks agreed to let her take piano lessons at home, even picking out a teacher for her. But after just a few lessons, Weeks flew into a rage and beat up the elderly piano teacher, accusing him of an affair with Patricia.

Eventually, Patricia had had enough and asked for a divorce. That request earned her a beating but she persisted and in 1968 the marriage was dissolved, with Patricia gaining the family home and car as part of the settlement.

Patricia did not enjoy her newfound freedom for long. In April 1968, her car was found abandoned at a local shopping center. She was never seen or heard from again.

Weeks remarried in 1971, a union that lasted until 1974 when he divorced Waunice Hinkle to be with a new love, Cynthia Jabour. By now, he'd sold his limo business and was living off the proceeds of a number of scams, most notably a phony stock scheme that netted him over a million dollars.

All was not well, though. Cynthia Jabour was beginning to understand why Weeks' previous partners had left him. She opted out of the relationship in the fall of 1980, agreeing to one last dinner with Weeks before they parted ways.

That date took place on October 5. The following day, Jabour's car was found abandoned in a casino parking lot. Weeks was questioned regarding her disappearance, even agreeing to a polygraph. Before the test could be carried out, he fled, moving first to Mexico and later to Chile.

In 1981, he was back in the United States, traveling on a Libyan passport in the name of "Robert Smith."

Settling in San Diego, he started a construction business. In 1983, while on a business trip to Colorado, he met 43-year-old divorcee Carol Ann Riley and persuaded her to join him in Southern California.

Like her predecessors, Riley soon tired of Weeks' obsessive jealousy. By 1986, she was planning on leaving him. On April 5 of that year, the couple went to dinner to discuss the break-up. Carol Riley's car was found abandoned in a hotel parking lot the following morning.

Weeks, meanwhile, had fled to Arizona, where he settled in Tucson and adopted the name, Charles Stolzenberg.

Just over a year later, in May 1987, the NBC program, "Unsolved Mysteries," aired an episode that featured a segment on Patricia Weeks' disappearance. The next morning, the station received a call from a woman who claimed that she was dating someone who strongly resembled the man featured in the program. The station passed on the information to police and Weeks was taken into custody on May 26, 1987.

In April 1988, Weeks was extradited to Nevada where he was convicted of murdering Patricia Weeks and Cynthia Jabour. He was sentenced to life imprisonment without the possibility of parole.

Weeks is still sought in California for the murder of Carol Ann Riley. In addition, he is the prime suspect in the disappearance of a former business partner, Jim Shaw.

Dorothy Williams

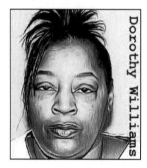

Despite a number of high-profile cases involving the likes of Aileen Wournos and Dorothea Puente, female serial killers are a rarity. Where they do exist they fall, most commonly, into three categories: parricides, who target their own family members; medical serial killers, who target patients under their care; and black widows, who attract and then murder wealthy spouses, for financial gain. In all cases, the most common method is poisoning, whether by toxic substance or by drug overdose. A female killer like Dorothy Williams, who bludgeoned, stabbed, and strangled her elderly victims to death, is therefore very rare.

There can be few killers as callous and calculating as Williams. The heroin-addicted murderer preyed on the most vulnerable of victims, talking her way into their homes on the pretense of needing a glass of water. Once inside, she'd turn on her frail target with extreme violence, beating, kicking, strangling, and stabbing them to death, then robbing them of their meager possessions.

Williams had already been victimizing and robbing the elderly for some time when she eventually turned to murder on December 5, 1987. On that day, police were called to the Chicago, Illinois, home of 79-year-old Lonnie Laws. They arrived to find the feeble, old man lying on the floor, a belt wrapped tightly around his neck. The apartment was in a state of disarray. Although there was no sign of forced entry, it was obvious that the motive for the murder had been robbery.

Almost a year to the day later, on December 6, 1988, police officers were summoned to an apartment building for the aged. On entering apartment 813, they were overwhelmed by an unbearable stench and soon located the decomposed body of 64-year-old Caesar Zuell. An autopsy would later reveal that he'd suffered three stab wounds to the chest, which had lacerated his lungs.

Although fingerprints had been lifted from both crime scenes, the police were no closer to making an arrest when another senior citizen fell prey to the brutal serial killer.

Mary Harris was 97 years old on the fateful afternoon of July 25, 1989, when she invited Dorothy Williams into her home in South Lake Park in Chicago. Williams had knocked on the door pleading poverty and Mrs. Harris had asked her to come inside so she could give her some money. As soon as the old woman's back was turned, Williams grabbed her by the neck, then throttled her to death with her own headscarf. The police would later find Mrs. Harris' battered body, both her eyes blackened from the beating she'd taken, the scarf still knotted around her throat. The apartment had been ransacked and several items, including a stereo, were missing.

This time, though, there was a witness. A neighbor, 71-year old Hubert Carmichael, reported that he'd seen a woman leaving the apartment at about 6:30 in the evening, carrying a box large enough to have held the missing stereo.

Despite this promising clue, the police had still not made an arrest by September 6, 1989, when Mr. Carmichael again contacted them. He said he'd seen the attacker again, standing at a bus stop near the apartment building. Officers rushed to the scene, and after Carmichael excitedly pointed her out, Dorothy Williams was taken into custody.

Faced with overwhelming forensic and eyewitness evidence against her, Williams did what most serial killers do in such circumstances, she tried to justify her actions. Mary Harris' death had been an accident, she said, while the two male victims had attacked her. She'd only been defending herself.

The police weren't buying it, and neither did the jury. On April 18, 1991, Williams was found guilty and sentenced to die by lethal injection. In 2003, Illinois governor, George Ryan, commuted her sentence to life without parole.

Douglas Franklin Wright

In September 1991, two young homeless men, Marty McDaniel and Tony Nelson, were approached in downtown Portland by a man offering them work outside the city. Keen to earn a few bucks, the men readily agreed and got into the man's red Toyota pickup, bearing Oregon license plates.

After a brief stop at the driver's apartment, the trio headed towards Mt. Hood. Leaving the highway, they then drove into the densely forested area that falls within the Warm Springs Indian Reservation. When the driver eventually brought the Toyota to a stop, Nelson walked from the vehicle with him, while McDaniel stood facing in the opposite direction. Suddenly McDaniel heard a gunshot. Turning towards the sound, he saw the driver holding a long-barreled revolver.

McDaniel sprinted for the cover of the trees, and kept running until he reached a highway. There, he flagged down motorist Ervie Dominguez. After listening to McDaniel's frantic story, Dominguez drove him to a rest area and phoned the police. While Dominguez was calling authorities, McDaniel slipped away.

Two days later, while detectives scoured the streets of downtown Portland for Marty McDaniel, hunters found the body of Tony Nelson. The following day, McDaniel was taken into custody.

Although he was originally considered a suspect, he was cleared once a man came forward to identify the driver of the red Toyota. His name was Douglas Franklin Wright, a two-time felon who had been convicted in 1964 for the murder of an Oregon woman and her mother. He'd served a ludicrously lenient 12 years for the double homicide.

The case resolved itself pretty quickly after that. McDaniel was able to pick Wright from a photo lineup and also led detectives to the apartment where he'd stopped off. Wright was registered as the tenant at the address and was also the registered owner of a Toyota pick-up. Meanwhile, ballistics tests showed that the weapon that had killed Tony Nelson had also killed another homeless man, Anthony Barker. His body had been discovered within one mile of where Nelson was found.

The next step was to obtain a search warrant for Wright's car and home. That search yielded two weapons, one of which was matched by ballistics to the bullets taken from Nelson and Barker.

Wright was charged with two counts of first-degree murder, although it would later transpire that the state of Oregon did not have jurisdiction over the Nelson murder. Nelson was a member of the Makah Tribe, and as his body had been found on the Warm Springs Indian Reservation, his murder was a federal matter.

Nonetheless, Oregon prosecutor's intended going ahead with the Barker prosecution. Then two additional charges were added to the docket when ballistics linked Wright's weapons to the deaths of two more homeless men.

Wright was convicted of all three murders on October 6, 1993, and sentenced to death. He refused to appeal his sentence. As his execution date approached he confessed to another crime, the 1984 abduction, sexual molestation, and murder of 10-year-old Luke Tredway.

Douglas Wright was executed by lethal injection on September 6, 1996, the first man to die in Oregon by this method.

For more True Crime books by Robert Keller please visit

http://bit.ly/kellerbooks

Made in the USA
Columbia, SC
03 December 2020

26217844R00093